M000118309

The
Random
House
Book of
Contemporary
Business
Letters

The Random House Book of

Contemporary Business Letters

Strategic Communications

Edited by
Stephen P. Elliott

Random House • New York

Library of Congress Cataloging-in-Publication Data

The Random House book of contemporary business letters/Strategic Communications; edited by Stephen P. Elliott.
   p. cm.
   "Adapted from The complete book of contemporary business letters" — T.p. verso.
   Includes indexes.
   ISBN 0-394-58170-9
   1. Business writing. 2. Commercial correspondence. 3. Letter-writing. I. Elliott, Stephen P. II. Strategic Communications, Inc. III. Title: Complete book of contemporary business letters. HF5718.3.R36 1989
   651.7'5 — dc20   89–8508

Manufactured in the United States of America

1 2 3 4 5 6 7 8 9

Contents

Communicating with the Sales Force

Research

Orders

Shipping

Statements

Quotations and Proposals

Contracts and Government Regulations

Chapter 2 ADVERTISING AND PUBLIC RELATIONS

Dealing with Advertising Agencies and Rate Requests

Announcements to Customers

Public Relations Companies and Fees

Chapter 3 CUSTOMER RELATIONS

Returned Checks

Payments and Returns by Customer

Chapter 4 HANDLING CUSTOMER COMPLAINTS

Complaint Justified

Complaint Unjustified

Chapter 5 CREDIT AND COLLECTIONS

Chapter 6 DEALING WITH SUPPLIERS

Problems

References

Employee Benefits

Job Descriptions and Evaluations

Chapter 8 MANAGING YOUR BUSINESS

Business Logistics

Business Plans, Help, and Housekeeping

Reservations and Rentals

Chapter 9 INTERNAL COMMUNICATIONS

Meetings and Planning

Suggestions, Reports, and Recommendations

Procedures and Policies

Preface

Many bright people, perhaps you're one of them, go to great lengths to avoid writing letters. Even when it means losing sales, alienating customers, or missing opportunities to present themselves in the best light, the threat of facing a blank page or a bare computer screen can be more powerful than the need to write a letter.

Just the thought of getting started can strike terror! "How should I open the letter?" "Just what information do I need to include?" "Am I communicating in the best tone for the situation and is my approach the most effective one?" "What closing will bring the action or reaction I want?" Sometimes the challenge of all these factors so overwhelms the writer that no letter at all is ever sent, or the letter that is finally composed misses the mark completely or subverts the writer's purpose.

All of this is most unfortunate because, in fact, armed with some simple guidelines to follow, and some excellent models from which to learn, business letter writing can be a relatively easy, extremely rewarding task.

Every piece of business correspondence is a sales tool. When you write to a customer, even about such a simple matter as confirming a delivery date, your correspondence is telling him about you and your company—about your professionalism, your interest in serving him, the style with which you conduct business. The same is true of an internal memo. Here your market is your associate, your boss, your subordinate. A weak or confusing communication represents you poorly, sending the message that you are inept or that you exercise poor judgment.

This book gives you your very own "file" of concise, crisp letters, memos, proposals and other business documents covering all of the major areas of business. Each one is designed to provide a model for effective communication. Of equal significance are the comments accompanying each document, which highlight the important features and help you to customize it.

Before you begin, decide whether you should be writing at all. This might seem like a foolish point, but it isn't. Writing is too time-consuming to engage in frivolously. The key question is "What do I want the reader to do after he or she reads this?" If you can't answer this question, you might reconsider whether you should write at all.

Don't **write** under the following conditions:

- When a quick phone call will do the job just as well as a letter, *and* a written record is *not* required.
- When you want to congratulate yourself. If your sole reason for writing is to let people know how great you are, think again. It's always better to *show* people you're competent than to tell them.
- When you're emotionally upset. If you're in a rage because someone on your staff failed to do what he was supposed to do, take some time to cool down before you begin to write. The letter will be better thought out, and you'll avoid saying things you may regret later on.

Do **write**, however, if any of the following apply:

- When the reader needs time to understand and absorb the message—for example, the material is complex and technical.
- When a permanent record is necessary to guard against misinterpretation or to protect the writer and the reader from the memory lapses that come with the passage of time.
- When you need a polite way to get someone's attention. For example, when you've been trying to reach a potential customer by phone, to no avail.
- When writing a letter can demonstrate that you've made a special effort.

Be prepared! It is impossible to write a well-reasoned letter or memo without preliminary thought. You need to focus on the decision maker, the person who will take action on what you are writing, and write with that person's needs in mind. Whether that person is a customer, a supplier, a creditor, a member of your staff, or your boss, aim your letter at the intended reader. The best way to achieve this is to picture the person in your mind as you write.

Get to the point. Establish what the main point of the letter is to be by asking yourself, "What is the one thing I want the reader to remember?" Start with a sentence that compels the reader to continue reading, and then quickly make the main point or points. Don't save important information for late in the document. Many readers will never get that far.

Be brief. If your letter is well organized, you won't be tempted to run on.

Most readers are just as busy as you are. They won't read pages and pages of explanation or analysis. Keep your letters, memos, and executive summaries to one page, if possible. Keep your paragraphs short.

Say what you mean. Hedging fools absolutely no one. Many people fall into the habit of qualifying their sentences in order to avoid categorical statements that may later be proven false. As a result, their documents are loaded with sentences starting with "There is a possibility that" or "There is some potential that." Lopping off these phrases will improve most prose. Use the active voice (he completed the project) rather than the passive voice (the project was completed by him) for the same reasons—it's shorter and more forthright.

Be positive. If you can state something positively, do so. Saying "We can't fill your order" is honest enough, but saying "We'd like to substitute Product X, a superior version of the product you ordered" is much better. People are much more receptive to the positive approach.

Be natural. Letter writing doesn't have the stilted, formal sound it once did. Don't use slang, but do write in a conversational style, similar to the way you speak. Even contractions like "I've" and "let's" accurately reflect the way people converse, and are perfectly acceptable in written communications today. People have been so used to Victorian phrasing in business correspondence that they find it hard to resist phrases like "Per your letter of August twenty-first" or "Enclosed herewith please find." Read your letter or memo aloud. If it sounds stiff, it probably is! Change it so that it sounds more natural.

How to Use This Book

This book provides an easy-to-access file of model letters for every category of business. Using the chapter openers as background and the comments accompanying the letters as a guide, you should find it easy to customize any document to suit your particular needs.

Accessing the letters. The documents fall within 10 major areas, or chapters, as spelled out in the table of contents, and then into more specific areas within each chapter. Each document has a descriptive title as well as a reference number, which identifies the chapter in which the letter can be found and, separated by a hyphen, its numerical placement within the chapter. In addition, there are two indexes from which to select the letter you need, one alphabetized by letter title and one by subject. After using the table of contents and indexes a few times you may find that, for your purposes, one of them proves more helpful to you than the others in locating the documents you want to use.

Customizing the letters. Once you've chosen the letter you wish to customize, you may want to make a copy of it on which you can do the editing. Keep the book open to that page, so you can refer to the original letter and the comments under it. The comments alert you to the important features of the letter—and assure that all essential information will be included.

In addition to the content of the model letters, pay particular attention to their tone and style. These factors determine the strength and effectiveness of your written communications.

Many of the letters and other documents in the book require very little customizing to make them appropriate for other situations, while some will need additional editing. The more complex letters provide excellent examples of how to handle particularly difficult situations.

When creating your own documents, consider combining paragraphs from several letters within the same category. This is particularly helpful when your needs fall somewhere between two model letters.

Review the letter when you finish to be sure you have changed all the information necessary to make the letter correct for your purposes. And, of course, proofread it to be sure there are no typographical errors or misspelled names.

Using Your Computer

The letters and other documents in *The Random House Book of Contemporary Business Letters* are available on computer disk for IBM-compatible and Macintosh computers. They are in text (ASCII) file for format, for use with virtually any word processor.

Using the disk, you can call up any letter from within your word processor, and customize and print it out quickly and easily.

Please turn to the handy bound-in envelope and order form for full information.

Sales and Marketing 1

Sales and marketing are the lifeblood of most companies. Written communications cover many different kinds of activities in these areas. All of them are crucial to the success of a company, primarily because they are directly responsible for generating income or, in the case of communicating with the sales force, dealing with those who generate the income. The effectiveness of the written word is critical in all of these endeavors.

Sales letters. Although all business communications should be persuasive, persuasion is usually the *sole* reason for sales letters. While a face-to-face encounter provides a sales person with the ability to establish rapport with the customer, sales letters long have proven themselves powerful marketing tools as well. They are personal, command undistracted attention and can be precisely targeted to a market. Methods have been developed over the years which, when followed, yield highly productive results.

The alternative to the salesman's warm smile and sincere handshake is the "grabber." It captures the reader's attention and gives him a compelling reason to continue reading. The headline or opening sentence should involve him immediately. Among the time-proven grabbers are free offers, announcements of new or improved products, provocative statements and attention-demanding questions.

The body of the letter should demonstrate a need and then show how your product or service meets that need. Next, persuade the reader to make a purchase decision. The easier you make that decision for him, the more successful the letter will be. A reduction of the selling price or offering a money-back guarantee are strong inducements to purchase. Finally, ask for action: mail the order card, phone today. Keep the ordering instructions simple and clear.

Follow-ups. The cardinal rule is always to leave a "thread" that leads to the next contact, to a continuation of the relationship. Ending a letter with "Please call me if you have an interest in any of our products" will seldom elicit action. Much better is "I will call you in a week to hear your reaction to this proposal." Imagine that the steps preceding a sale are a dance and that you are leading.

Following up also means thanking people who give you leads or information about potential customers. Report your progress to date, if appropriate, and always let them know if you make the sale. It's simple courtesy.

Communicating with the sales force. Because most salespeople are on the road or unavailable, managers must communicate with them by memo or letter. The key is to be straightforward and to use a civil tone. Salespeople are no less sensitive to nuances than any other human beings. With their distance from the office, they may be prone to misunderstanding communications that aren't carefully worded.

Orders and shipping. Orders and shipping issues are part of the sales process in many organizations, since the salesperson will often also be responsible for fulfillment. The touchstone is to be pleasant and honest, particularly if there are difficulties in fulfilling the order.

Proposals, bids and quotations. Whether writing proposals, confirming terms, or changing terms and specifications, these letters have contractual ramifications. You may want to have them looked at by an attorney if significant amounts of money are involved. As with all customer correspondence, be clear, concise and polite.

Company Name
Address
City, State Zip

Date

Mr. and Mrs. Ned Hawkins
59 Winter Street
Easton, MD 21601

Dear Mr. and Mrs. Hawkins:

Congratulations on your new home and welcome to the Easton area! We wish you many happy years in this new location.

We at Chim, Chim, Cheree have been serving customers in Easton for over 50 years, and we would like to add your name to our list of satisfied customers. We are specialists in chimney cleaning, damper repair, masonry repair, and chimney cap installation. Please call me at 281-5333 to arrange an appointment for a **complimentary** fireplace inspection and consultation with one of the professionals from our staff. I've included our brochure, which tells you more about our company and services.

Again, welcome to Easton. I look forward to hearing from you.

Sincerely,

George Kendry

Enclosure

- Explain who you are and the services you provide.

- If possible, give an incentive for the customer to try your services (premium, discount, complimentary visit, etc.).

- Clearly indicate how you may be reached.

Company Name
Address
City, State Zip

Date

J & J Catering
103 Shady Lane
Nesconset, NY 11767

Dear Ms. Johnson:

Thank you for choosing AAAble Rents for your first catering job. I heard that it was a great success. The staff and I wish you and Mrs. Jones the best success with your new service.

At AAAble, we are ready when you need us. In addition to chairs, tables, china, silverware, table linens, and glasses, which you have already rented from us, we can also supply you with tents, candelabra, hollowware, party decorations, dance floors, and many other party supplies. Please call us soon!

Best regards,

John Miller
President

- Thank them for the business.

- Offer any additional services that you might have.

- Solicit more business.

Company Name
Address
City, State Zip

Date

Mr. John Siegler
Edge Tech
118 Collen's Ferry Road
Abbeyville, SC 29620

Dear Mr. Siegler:

Thank you for your order of last Tuesday; we appreciate new clients, as they are the lifeblood of our business. I am enclosing our latest company brochure, which describes our capabilities and terms of sale. I think you will find the section on small motors particularly interesting.

Our regional sales representative, Chuck James, will contact you next week to set up an appointment. At that time he can explain our products more fully and answer any questions you might have.

We look forward to serving you again.

Very truly yours,

Fred Spaninger
Vice-President, Sales

Enclosure

- Thank them for the business.

- Explain what you have enclosed and why.

- Establish the mechanism for doing more business with the customer, whether by mail, phone, or in person.

Company Name
Address
City, State Zip

Date

Mr. John Zimmerman
14 Sachem Village
West Lebanon, NH 03784

Dear Mr. Zimmerman:

Thank you for your order for carving chisels. You'll find that our tools will enhance your work and pleasure in woodworking. They are well-crafted, enduring, useful, and unique—the best that money can buy.

I'm enclosing a copy of our latest catalog. We have expanded into gardening tools in addition to our line of woodworking tools.

We look forward to hearing from you again soon.

Very truly yours,

Jason Sanderson
Vice-President, Customer Service

Enclosure

- Express appreciation for the business.

- Explain anything new or different in your catalog.

- Say that you're looking forward to doing more business.

Company Name
Address
City, State Zip

Date

Mr. and Mrs. John Farrell
3798 Canterbury Road
Cleveland Heights, OH 44118

Dear John and Fran:

It was a pleasure meeting you last week, and I thank you for the opportunity to introduce you to our insurance plans. I hope you have had the chance to look over the information on family protection, retirement income, and education plan that I left with you.

I will call you Thursday evening to see if you have any questions about our services. I hope to have the opportunity to work with you in planning your family's financial security and other insurance needs.

Sincerely yours,

Samuel T. Gold
Account Executive

- Thank them for the initial meeting.

- Establish a time when you will next contact them (at which time you can try to set up a meeting to close the sale).

Company Name
Address
City, State Zip

Date

Mr. Fred Johns
Kiddie Korner, Inc.
20 World Trade Center, Suite 3557
New York, NY 10048

Dear Mr. Johns:

It was a pleasure meeting with you last Friday. I'm glad we had the opportunity to discuss and, I hope, resolve some of the problems you had with our toy shipments three years ago. As I mentioned, we've upgraded our delivery system in the past year, which should prevent any reccurrence of late shipments and shipping errors.

I will call you in two weeks, after you've had the chance to look over our new catalog.

We look forward to doing business with you again.

Sincerely,

Adam Woodruff
Vice President, Sales

- Express appreciation for the client/customer's time.

- Follow up with what you discussed during the sales call (answer questions raised, send material requested, etc.). If the customer stopped doing business with you because he or she was dissatisfied, state how the problem has been, or can be, fixed.

- Always leave a thread—a link to your next contact.

Company Name
Address
City, State Zip

Date

Mr. and Mrs. M. F. Dudley
42 Summit Drive
Whittier, CA 90605

Dear Toni and Marshall:

Because of the rapid appreciation of housing (and replacement costs) here in Southern California, we need to make sure your current homeowner's policy of $300,000 provides sufficient protection before we renew the policy on May 30. We are generally suggesting that our accounts increase their policies 10-15%.

If you've made significant improvements to your house in the last year, you'll need to think about an additional increase to the policy amount.

I'll call you next week to discuss your coverage.

Best wishes,

James Bowman

- If you're seeking additional business or an increase in an account, be sure to give a reason that makes sense to your reader.

- Leave the ball in your court—"I'll call you..." is much more appealing to a busy customer than "please call me."

Company Name
Address
City, State Zip

Date

Mrs. Betty Tovar
2030 Ocean Drive
Hallandale, FL 33009

Dear Mrs. Tovar:

We were sorry to see that your name has not been on our list for service contract renewals for the past two years. If you have had a problem with Friendly Air Conditioning, we would like to remedy it.

We have also expanded and improved our service fleet in the past year, and our prices have remained very competitive. We now have servicemen on call 24 hours a day and can guarantee that one will be at your place within an hour of your call.

I'll telephone you next week to see if I can answer any questions you might have about our new services. We would very much like to welcome you back as a Friendly Air Conditioning customer.

Sincerely,

David C. Hunter
Customer Service Representative

Enclosure

- Highlight any improvements in your products or services that have occurred since you last did business.

- Try to find out why they stopped doing business with you.

- Let them know that you would like their business back.

Company Name
Address
City, State Zip

Date

Mr. Donald Green
Green Ink Printers
2407 Halburton Road
Beachland, OH 44119

Dear Mr. Green:

Thank you for your request for more information on American
Adjustable Frequency AC Motor Speed Control products.

American has been producing quality AC motor controls since 1974,
and we have over 14,000 units in operation throughout the world. We
have an excellent reputation for quality, reliability, and service, and all
our products are designed, engineered, and manufactured in the U.S.A.

I've enclosed a catalog that describes our products. Please contact me
for more sales information and application assistance. I would like to be
of further service to you.

Again, thank you for your interest in American Controls.

Sincerely yours,

Joseph G. Gest
Sales Manager

Enclosure

- Express thanks for their interest in your product or services.

- Let them know you're interested in providing more information and try to find out more
  about what they're looking to buy.

Company Name
Address
City, State Zip

Date

Mr. Michael Handel
178 Pugsley Avenue
Brooklyn, NY 11201

Dear Mr. Handel:

May I use your name when prospective clients ask for a reference?
You have been a valued client for over ten years, and you are well-
known and respected as a piano teacher in our community—a perfect
reference for a piano-tuning business!

I will call you in a few days for your answer. Thank you very much.

Sincerely,

Jason Russell

- Express how you appreciate their business.

- Make it sound like an honor and privilege to be "selected" as a reference. (Saying complimentary things usually helps.)

- Arrange to follow up.

Company Name
Address
City, State Zip

Date

Mr. and Mrs. Jonathan Walker
3500 Falmouth Road
Shaker Heights, OH 44122

Dear Mr. and Mrs. Walker:

Thank you very much for allowing us to use you as a reference for prospective clients interested in our window-washing service. We appreciate your time and value you as a client. As a token of our appreciation, I have enclosed a coupon good for 10% off our regular rates for our next visit.

Again, thank you.

Sincerely,

Orville Bruno

Enclosure

- Express your appreciation for the referral permission and for their business.

- When possible, include some token of appreciation for the use of their name.

Company Name
Address
City, State Zip

Date

Dear Homeowner:

Now that fall is here and you are getting things ready for the winter, it's time to think about your driveway. Does your driveway have cracks? Is it in need of sealing?

East Coast Seal Cote Co. specializes in asphalt driveway refurbishing. We seal cracks, large and small, and apply two coats of premium rubberized sealer to the entire surface. Our finish is guaranteed for two years.

If you would like a free, no-obligation estimate, please call 572-7800. You don't even have to be home for the estimate; we will leave it in your mailbox.

We look forward to helping your driveway look better and last longer.

Yours very truly,

Mark Bretton
Vice President, Sales

- Explain your services.

- Make it easy for them to respond.

- Ask for action—a response, an order.

Company Name
Address
City, State Zip

Date

Dear Maintenance Manager:

- Do you have concrete floors in your manufacturing area?

- Do they require maintenance in heavy traffic areas due to cracking?

- Would you like to end this maintenance headache?

If your answer is yes to these three questions, we suggest that you try Glass-Coat brand sealer/resurfacer. Glass-Coat is a reinforced polycarbonate coating that goes on like paint and stands up even to heavy forklift traffic. It resists most chemicals and is nontoxic in the event of a fire.

We feel so strongly that once you try Glass-Coat you'll want it in all your problem areas that we will send you a free sample to use as a test. If this sounds good, give me a call at 1-800-976-3871 for the name of our representative in your area.

Sincerely,

Tony Regalus
Vice President, Sales

- Explain your product.

- Direct it to the most likely buying influence.

- Ask for a response.

SPRING CLEANUP

Dread cleaning up your yard this spring? We will do it for you at a price you can't afford to pass up!

Full cleanup: Rake out entire lawn; rake out dead grass, leaves, branches and debris from garden and flower beds; clean all lawn and driveway areas and pile debris neatly at the curb for city pickup.

Small-average lot	$60-75
Larger than average or small corner lot	$85-150
Large corner lot	$150-up
X-large lot	Call for estimate

Mini cleanup: Same work done as above except no beds are touched. Cost is 1/2 to 3/4 of above prices, depending on size of lot and lawn area.

For quick, reliable service, please call
Steve, Pete, or Joe Jetson
39 Provinceline Road
Princeton, NJ 08540
(609) 924-0111

All work done on first-come, first-served basis. References available upon request. Gift certificates available.

- Outline your services and quote typical rates.

- Make sure they know who to contact and where you can be reached.

- Distribute widely and frequently in targeted area.

Company Name
Address
City, State Zip

Name Our New Ice Cream Sundae Sensation!

Come in and taste our latest ice cream treat, a luscious concoction of mango, papaya, and coconut ice cream topped with chocolate and pineapple sauces, whipped cream, and candied grapefruit bits. Then dream up a name for this sundae sensation and fill out one of our entry forms.

If your entry is selected, you win a $25 gift certificate available for use at any one of our three Robert's Ice Cream Parlor locations: Landsdowne Square (downtown), West Road Mall, or South Landsdowne.

Hurry! The contest ends June 5. Be a winner, name a winner!

- Outline contest rules, deadlines, and awards.

- Contest should be geared to promote your business traffic (e.g., involve people coming to your store).

Company Name
Address
City, State Zip

Date

Mr. and Mrs. Ken Humphries
78 Fairview Road
North Branford, CT 06471

Dear Mr. and Mrs. Humphries:

This year we are again offering to our customers our prepayment option of a 5% cash discount on our seasonal mowing contract (April through November). Many of our customers prefer the seasonal mowing contract because of the convenience of writing one check and using one stamp.

If you decide to take advantage of this offer, please send us your check for $171.00 for the full year's mowing by April 30. If you decide to pay monthly, the seasonal charge will total $180.00.

If you have any questions concerning prepayment or your cost, please call me at 484-9333.

Sincerely,

Brian Victor

- State clearly the advantages and terms (including deadline of the offer) of the discount.

- Encourage your customers to call you directly. Giving a person's name is always better than saying "please call our office."

Company Name
Address
City, State Zip

Date

Mr. and Mrs. Frank Long
590 Farragut Hills Boulevard
Knoxville, TN 37920

Dear Mr. and Mrs. Long:

As a special offer to new customers, we will clean your living room, dining room, and hall carpets for a flat fee of $49.95. And that's not all—we will also clean any one of your bedroom carpets **at no added cost.** This offer is good through May 31.

We are extending this low, low price to you to demonstrate the fine quality of work we do, with the hope that you will join the list of the many satisfied customers we service.

I've enclosed a description of our company, our services, and our regular rates. You may be particularly interested in quotes from some of your Farragut Hills neighbors (p. 3 of the brochure). Please take a minute to call me at 773-4592 and schedule an appointment. I'm sure you'll be very satisfied.

Sincerely,

Jim Ballard

Enclosure

- Outline your offer clearly. People are very skeptical about offers like this and you must be very explicit.

- If you can get testimonials, use them in your promotional literature and refer to them in the letter.

Company Name
Address
City, State Zip

Ameritherm Temperature Controls invites you to the National Plastics Exposition and to the windy city of Chicago on November 2 and 3. You can view the full range of our temperature controllers for plastics manufacturing equipment at our company display in:

Booth number 164, 2nd floor of McCormick East

Our product specialists and sales representatives will be on hand to answer any questions you might have.

Our temperature controllers are also installed on the extruders in the following manufacturers' booths:

Davis Standard	Booth number 27
Wellex	Booth number 53
NRM	Booth number 71
Husky	Booth number 82
Glouster	Booth number 99
HPM	Booth number 125

We look forward to seeing you.

- Indicate what products you have on display.

- If your booth is in a difficult-to-find location, provide directions or a map.

- If your product is also part of other equipment at the show, indicate where it can be found (name of company and booth location).

Company Name
Address
City, State Zip

Date

Dear Beachwood Resident:

The Frameworks is opening a new store in the Beachwood Mall on June 1. To celebrate and to welcome you to our new store, bring in this letter and we'll take 25% off any ready-made frame or 15% off any custom frame you purchase before July 15.

We specialize in all kinds of metal, wood, and plastic frames and have over 300 different styles to choose from in our store.

Please stop in and see us soon.

Sincerely,

Susan Weston
Store Manager

- Make sure you can determine how the person heard of your offer (so you can determine the effectiveness of the campaign).

- Offer some enticement for responding quickly.

Company Name
Address
City, State Zip

Date

Ms. Theresa S. Rouse
Conference Coordinator
Southeast Venture Corporation
2000 21st Avenue South
Nashville, TN 37212

Dear Ms. Rouse:

If you are looking for a truly unique spouse activities program for your national sales conference in June, I believe my workshop, "The Beauty of Ikebana" (Japanese flower arranging), would provide a memorable experience.

The four-hour workshop offers insight into the meaning of particular ikebana arrangements, the history of the flowering arranging art in Japan, and an opportunity for participants to make and take home a small arrangement of fresh flowers. I bring to the workshop several arrangements to illustrate examples of different styles.

I've enclosed a brochure with color photographs, a description of my experience and education in ikebana, a client list, and a fee schedule to give you a better idea of what I can offer you. I will call you next week to discuss your program needs and answer any questions you may have.

Sincerely,

Silvia Platt

Enclosure

- Tie your seminar to a result the reader wants—i.e., an interesting and memorable program.

- Include supporting information (brochures, etc.) to give details and arrange to follow up.

Company Name
Address
City, State Zip

Date

To: Boston Area Foodwell Stores

For the Fourth of July this year, we will be running a special promotion on O'Grady's "Fire Breathing Barbeque Sauce." There will be a special point-of-sale display, coupons in the local papers, and radio advertising. This sauce has done well in test markets in New Hampshire and Virginia and should help sell chicken and pork in addition to beef.

The program will run from May 21 to July 9. We hope to move 40,000 bottles in this time period. Our sales representative, Dean Phillips, will contact you next week to give you further details of the program and to answer any questions you might have.

Sincerely,

Frank Hogan
Vice President, Marketing

- Explain the elements of the sales program.

- State the duration and objectives of the program.

- Indicate who the contact person is for the program.

Company Name
Address
City, State Zip

Date

To: Lumi-Co Distributors

Lumi-Co is pleased to announce the expansion of last year's growth program to include our new line of indoor and outdoor sodium lighting.

The program will run throughout this year and has a quarterly discount that gets better as the year progresses—provided you meet the agreed-upon sales levels. Our sales representative will be contacting you to review the details of this plan. Together we can make this year a "bright" year for everyone!

Yours very truly,

Vincent Cusano
Vice President, Sales

- Explain how the program works and what is included.

- State the duration of the program.

- Solicit participation.

Company Name
Address
City, State Zip

To: All Chicago Area Managers of Billie Burger Restaurants

From: Ray Hanson, Promotion Manager

Date:

Subject: Spring/Summer Advertising Campaign

We are starting our Billie's Better Burger campaign in your area on April 21. This will coincide with national TV advertising during the Monday night baseball games.

The primary advertising in your area will be on WQOX and WNNB radio stations, as well as weekly ads and coupons in the Chicago Tribune.

We expect excellent response to this program, so plan your supplies accordingly. The program will run through June 30.

Let us know if there are any questions. Please have the weekly coupon totals ready to report with your weekly sales figure. Thank you and good luck!

- State when the campaign starts and ends.

- Describe how the advertising will be done; clearly state what actions you expect of the recipient of the letter.

- Have a feedback mechanism to record the success of your program.

Company Name
Address
City, State Zip

Date

Dear Distributor:

Frampton Gear Reducers is embarking on a large-scale advertising campaign for its new line of offset parallel gear reducers. We are targeting primarily the paper, stone and gravel, and chemical industries. We will be running full-page ads in *Chemical Age, Pulp and Paper Digest,* and *Gravel and Trap Rock News.* We will also be running similar advertising in *Power Design.* Ads will start in June and run through December.

We will make reprints available that are suitable for imprinting and mailing to your customers. We hope that this will stir up a lot of leads, and we are ready to help you close orders.

Good luck and good selling!

Yours very truly,

Bill Johnson
Vice President, Marketing

- Indicate who is targeted.

- State what advertising vehicle(s) will be used.

- Describe how long the program is to last.

Company Name
Address
City, State Zip

Date

Dear Customer:

We at North Shore Home Remodeling have been known for the past seven years for our excellent craftsmanship. Last year—the best in our history—more than 200 homeowners became North Shore customers. We look forward to continuing to serve the five towns on the North Shore.

This spring, we are expanding and will be starting our new division, North Shore Aluminum Siding, Refinishing, and Brick Cleaning. I'm enclosing a brochure that explains our new products and services. If you have been pleased with a remodeled kitchen or bath that we've built for you, you will love the way we can make the exterior of your home look brand new. Please call us at 790-6345 for a no-obligation consultation and quotation.

Sincerely,

Bruno Patella
President

Enclosure

- Establish the quality of your present product/service.

- Explain your new product/service.

- Make a tie between the old and the new product/service.

- Ask for action (quote, meeting, or order).

Company Name
Address
City, State Zip

To: Field Sales

From: Ken Daggs, Marketing Manager

Date:

Subject: Price Increase

On May 1, Powerflo will announce a 7 1/2% price increase on all plastic pumps and a 9 1/2% increase on the combination plastic/cast-iron pumps, effective June 1. Both prices are the result of increased PVC prices.

Orders entered before June 1 with shipment dates prior to July 1 will be priced at the old levels, and any orders entered after May 31 will be increased accordingly.

Please call me if you have any questions.

- Give as much advance notice as possible for a price increase, since the salespeople will want to prepare their customers.

- Give the amount of the price change, the date it will take effect, and a brief reason that salespeople can use with their customers.

Company Name
Address
City, State Zip

To: All Sales Reps

From: Ron Bryant, Marketing Manager

Date:

Subject: Power Mate Gear Reducers

Starting with shipments in June, all Power Mate gear reducers will have new and improved shaft seals. We have made the popular double lip seal standard across the line. This superior sealing system stands up to tough applications two and a half times better than the previous single lip seal systems.

We are offering this added feature at no additional cost. Please use the attached data sheet to explain the features and benefits of this new seal to your customers. We will be happy to help you work through any non-standard applications.

Thank you for your support. Please call me if you have any questions.

Attachment

- Tell how the product has changed and how to apply the change to get sales.

- Solicit feedback and offer further assistance.

Company Name
Address
City, State Zip

To: Field Sales

From: Ben Poole, National Sales Manager

Date:

Subject: Fred Porter Joins Our Team

It is with great pleasure that I introduce our newest sales engineer, Fred Porter. Fred has an extensive background in computer systems, particularly in positioning systems software.

Fred and his wife, Barbara, will be relocating to Richmond, where he will be joining our Southern office, handling accounts in Virginia, Kentucky, North Carolina, and South Carolina starting July 1.

Welcome aboard, Fred!

- Emphasize introduction in subject line.

- Give a short description of the person's background.

- Say when and where the person will locate.

Company Name
Address
City, State Zip

To: Tom Anderson

From: Bill Strejata, Regional Sales Manager

Date:

Subject: New Territory Assignment

As you know, Jim Fitzpatrick is leaving us next month, which will leave us one person short in the Boston office. I am asking you to assume responsibility for part of his territory, specifically southern New Hampshire, for the time being.

Please get together with Jim before he leaves. He and I have discussed the transition, and he plans to allow enough time so that he can introduce you to all his major accounts. I want you to make especially sure that we have a smooth transition of the Milekin Company account. We have spent a lot of time and effort developing this account, and we want to pass the baton with professional grace.

I will be in your office next Friday to see how things are going. We have every faith that you will handle this new territory in your usual highly professional manner. Good luck!

- Smooth transitions are vital to keeping customer goodwill. Give specific direction; ensure that the outgoing rep and the newly assigned rep talk to each other, and follow up.

Company Name
Address
City, State Zip

To: All Salesmen

From: Bob Potter, National Sales Manager

Date:

Subject: Fourth Quarter Bonus Bonanza

The last quarter of the year is traditionally our slowest quarter. To make things more exciting this year, we are offering an expanded bonus program. For orders placed in the fourth quarter, we will pay sales representatives an additional 1% commission on orders for immediate shipment. All product categories qualify, and bonus payments will be made on December 15th!

Get out there, stir up sales, and earn a nice Christmas bonus.

• Be specific about how the bonus works and to what products it applies. Also state time frames, limitations, and when the bonus will be paid.

Company Name
Address
City, State Zip

To: Jim Watson, Eastern Regional Sales Manager

From: Allen Beck, Marketing Manager

Date:

Subject: Second Quarter Performance

I've been reviewing your region's performance, and last quarter it was excellent! Certainly, 115% of plan is an outstanding result.

Your team posted over-plan sales in all product categories but two—chain and line. Is there a reason why these two groups were only 87% and 71% of plan respectively? I'll be in your area the first week of next month and would like to have dinner with you to discuss how we can help you get these two products on track.

My secretary will call yours to arrange a date.

- Be specific when you're talking about performance—generalized platitudes don't motivate anyone.

- Congratulate good performance first; suggest corrective actions for areas that need improvement later on.

- Take a problem-solving, rather than a punitive, approach.

Company Name
Address
City, State Zip

Date

Dear Executive:

We need the information requested in the enclosed questionnaire in order to prepare <u>The Marketer's Reference Guide</u>. Please take a minute and help us.

The Marketer's Reference Guide is a resource book highlighting the multitude of marketing and support services that businesses use in the greater Phoenix area. It's a valuable reference for your company because it indexes the local talent available to meet your marketing needs.

Whether your organization is in the market for direct-mail consulting, graphic-design help, a brochure writer, or an advertising/marketing agency, you can find what you need by looking through the 162 different categories of suppliers of services in this book.

We will send you future editions of The Marketer's Reference Guide free-of-charge if you return the questionnaire by September 30. Alerting us to your needs (by filling out and returning the questionnaire) will also enable us to invite you to specific trade shows geared to your interests.

Thanks for taking the time to complete and return the enclosed questionnaire. We promise that you will be the ultimate beneficiary.

Sincerely,

Marsha Becker
Editor-in-Chief

Enclosure

P.S. If you would like an additional copy of The Marketer's Reference Guide or need additional copies for other departments, you may order them for $19.95 ($10.00 off the cover price of $29.95) simply by enclosing with this questionnaire a check made payable to The Marketer's Reference Guide.

- It's very difficult to get people to return questionnaires. (Some people go so far as to enclose dollar bills with their requests.) Here the offer is a free reference book and invitation to trade shows.

- The P.S. will get read—and may get sales even if the questionnaire isn't filled out.

Company Name
Address
City, State Zip

Date

Mr. Robert Swan
2823 East Cudia
Phoenix, AZ 85018

Dear Mr. Swan:

Thank you for the information you provided for our 1988-1989 marketing campaigns questionnaire. As always, your cooperation has helped ensure the success of this project.

Your copy of the findings is enclosed. Please note that some of this information is extremely sensitive and should be treated as confidential.

We'll be back to request an update in September. In the meantime, we welcome any changes or corrections, which we will incorporate in our July newsletter.

Sincerely,

Brian Patenaude

Enclosure

- Questionnaires are marketing tools. Providing results to respondents rewards them for participation and gives you another chance to get their attention. People who have a long history of cooperation should be thanked and commended, even in a form letter.

Company Name
Address
City, State Zip

Dear Customer:

Thank you for visiting The Stork's Baby recently. I hope you found what you were looking for and that you were satisfied with the quality and the variety of baby products in our store.

Please help us by completing and returning this survey about our salespeople so that we can continue to improve the quality of our service. It is very short and will only take a few minutes of your time. Thank you very much for your help.

Sincerely yours,

Joanne Wright
Manager

Did a salesperson wait on you within a reasonable amount of time?
    [ ] Yes   [ ] No

Was the salesperson knowledgeable about the merchandise?
    [ ] Very   [ ] Somewhat   [ ] Not at all

Were you treated with courtesy?
    [ ] Yes   [ ] No

Did the salesperson mention:
        Our Free Special Order Service?   [ ] Yes   [ ] No
        Our Shower Planning Service?   [ ] Yes   [ ] No

Overall, how would you rate your salesperson at The Stork's Baby?
    [ ] Excellent   [ ] Good   [ ] Average   [ ] Poor

Any suggestions or comments regarding our salespeople?

_____

_____

If anyone was particularly helpful, please let us know.

_____

_____

- Explain how the feedback you receive will help you improve the quality of the salesforce.

- Mention any special services which may have been overlooked.

- Thank the customer for his or her time and assistance.

Company Name
Address
City, State Zip

Date

Mr. Hiram Kerlinsky
Kerlinsky Auto Parts
73 Noble Avenue
Longmeadow, MA 01006

Dear Mr. Kerlinsky:

In reviewing our accounts we noticed that we have not received any orders from your store for our Maxi-Pipes Chrome Exhaust kit during the last six months. In the preceding year, you had ordered an average of 10 kits per month. Naturally, we hate to lose a steady customer.

It's important to us that we keep informed of our customers' degree of satisfaction with our products and service so we can continue to serve them well. It's particularly important that we learn why old customers no longer order from us.

Won't you please help us by completing the following questionnaire and returning it to us in the enclosed stamped envelope? It will only take a minute and your answers will help us provide better services in the future.

Thank you for your time, and we hope you'll be placing an order with us soon.

Sincerely,

August Henry
Sales Manager

Why did you stop ordering Maxi-Pipes Chrome Exhausts? (Check all that apply.)
        [ ] Dissatisfied with quality of product
        [ ] Dissatisfied with promptness of delivery
        [ ] Dissatisfied with payment terms
        [ ] Experienced customer service problems
        [ ] Other (Please explain.)

_____

_____

What will it take to get your business back?

_____

_____

- Ask direct questions—you'd be surprised at what people will tell you. Besides, you have nothing to lose.

- Express interest in getting the business back.

Company Name
Address
City, State Zip

Thank you for stopping by our booth at the Cleveland Outdoor Expo. Would you please help us by completing the following survey? As you'll see, it's a brief one and will only take a minute or two to complete. Then, either hand it to one of our sales representatives in our booth or place it in the attached return envelope and drop it in the mail. No postage is required.

Your answers are important because we analyze the information to help us learn more about our customers and their desires and to provide better products in the future.

Again, thank you for your time and your interest.

SPIFFY CYCLES CUSTOMER SURVEY

1. Name:_____
    Address: _____

2. Date:

3. Why did you stop by our booth?
    [ ] Looking to buy a bicycle [ ] Attracted by display
    [ ] Spiffy's reputation   [ ] Other (please specify)

4. Have you ever heard of Spiffy before? [ ] Yes   [ ] No

5. If so, where?
    [ ] Owned one before   [ ] Friend/relative
    [ ] TV/magazine ad   [ ] Saw in store
    [ ] Other (please specify)

6. Based on what you have seen and heard, would you buy a Spiffy cycle?
    [ ] Yes   [ ] No

7.   Are you interested in a bicycle for yourself or for someone else?
       [ ] Self   [ ] Other adult   [ ] Child

8.   Have you ever owned a bicycle?
       [ ] Yes   [ ] No

9.   Birthdate: _____

10.   Marital status: [ ] Married   [ ] Single

11.   Occupation: _____

12.   Age of each child living at home: _____, _____, _____, _____

13.   Which group describes your family income?
       [ ] Under $15,000   [ ] $35,001-$45,000
       [ ] $15,000-$25,000   [ ] $45,001-$55,000
       [ ] $25,001-$35,000   [ ] Over $55,000

14. Which of the following credit cards do you use regularly?
       [ ] Bank (Visa, MC)   [ ] American Express, Diners Club
       [ ] Gas, department store [ ] None of these

- Express appreciation for filling out the questionnaire and let them know why the information is valuable.

- Indicate how easy it is to complete the questionnaire and to return it.

- Make sure the questionnaire *is* easy to fill out.

Company Name
Address
City, State Zip

Date

Mr. Conrad Sullivan
Sullivan Consulting Company
213 Riverway
Boston, MA 02215

Dear Mr. Sullivan:

Thank you for your recent order (PO #437-B) of stationery from The Inky Printing Company. We are currently processing your order for 2,000 letterheads, 1,000 second sheets, and 1,000 envelopes. I expect your order to be ready within the next two weeks; we will notify you when it is ready for pick-up.

Again, thank you for doing business with us.

Sincerely,

Joseph T. Fries

- Express your appreciation for the order.

- State each item of the order and, if possible, the expected date when it will be ready.

- Make sure you follow up as promised.

Company Name
Address
City, State Zip

Date

Mr. Roger G. Jackson
Sugar & Spice & Something Nice Co.
Beachwood Mall
Beachland, OH 44119

Dear Mr. Jackson:

Thank you for ordering 10 cases of Cajun Cooking Magic spices. Your order (PO #S-43CC) is being shipped via the Package Express Company (Bill of Lading #IG46P00L) and should arrive in 7-10 days (their estimate). I've enclosed an invoice for the spices. I hope I can be of further service to you.

Sincerely,

Frank T. Beck
Sales Representative

Enclosure

- Express appreciation for the order.

- Detail what was ordered, who is shipping it, and when it is expected to arrive (if possible). Include all relevant purchase order and shipping numbers in case there are problems later.

Company Name
Address
City, State Zip

Date

Mrs. Amy Rowland
54 Lincoln Street
Glen Ridge, NJ 07028

Dear Mrs. Rowland:

Thank you for your recent order of a "Christine" doll from Dreamgirls.
As you know, our dolls are handmade in West Germany.
Unfortunately, orders for "Christine" dolls this Christmas season have
surpassed our expectations, and the doll is out of stock at the moment.
We expect another shipment of dolls in two weeks, and as soon as it
arrives, we will ship the doll to you via express mail, at our expense, so
that your little girl will not be disappointed on Christmas morning.

I'm sorry for the inconvenience, and I thank you for your understanding.

Sincerely yours,

Henry D. Krieger

- Apologize, give the reason for the delay and, if possible, let the customer know when to expect delivery.

- Show the customer you care about the order by going out of your way—in this case, Express Mail—to expedite delivery.

Company Name
Address
City, State Zip

Date

Mr. Robert Somes
900 West Rahn Road
Dayton, OH 45449

Dear Mr. Somes:

I am returning your check for $153.00 because we no longer make the foul-weather gear (item G357) you ordered. I'm sorry to disappoint you, but that item has not been available for over six months now. We do make several other styles of foul-weather gear, and I hope you'll find one of these new styles, pictured in our new catalog that I've enclosed, to your liking.

I hope we can be of further service to you.

Very truly yours,

Jeff Downing

Enclosure

- Express empathy that the merchandise ordered is not available.

- If payment has been made, explain how you've dealt with it (returning their check, crediting their account, etc.).

- Offer comparable alternative merchandise if available.

Company Name
Address
City, State Zip

Date

Mr. William Skillins
29 New Street
Port Monmouth, NJ 07758

Dear Mr. Skillins:

Thank you for ordering the ski mask (item no. 69M) from our catalog. However, we are unable to process your order because you didn't indicate your color choice. The ski mask comes in red, navy blue, and black.

Please call me at (800) 495-5000 with your preference, so I can send you your ski mask as soon as possible.

Sincerely yours,

Lance Handel

- Explain why you're unable to process the order.

- If a corrective measure needs to be taken before the order can be processed, detail what needs to be done and who is to do it.

Company Name
Address
City, State Zip

Date

Mr. Anthony Santos
Ace Dance Troupe
80 Broadway
Massapequa Park, NY 11758

Dear Mr. Santos:

The 15 beige grass skirts, silver tops, and headdresses that you asked us to make for you are finished, and I've shipped them to you by UPS, insured. You should be receiving them around July 28.

I'm enclosing our invoice #4219 for the order, which totals $672.50, including shipping costs. Thank you again for your order; I look forward to providing you with other costumes in the future.

Best wishes,

Leilani Lahaina
Manager

Enclosure

- Indicate what is being shipped and when delivery is expected.

- Include the invoice number and amount, plus any other relevant information.

- Solicit future business.

Company Name
Address
City, State Zip

Date

Dr. Charles Friedman
Ring Medical Center
67 Main Street
Belchertown, MA 01007

Dear Dr. Friedman:

We've received the 25 boxes of No. 2 rubber gloves (Purchase Order #12-8945J) that were backordered, and I am sending them to you by Jetline Air Freight (shipment #22-B-6732). They should arrive within a week.

I'm sorry for the problems this delay may have caused you. We look forward to serving you again soon.

Sincerely,

Paul T. White
Customer Service

- Indicate what is being shipped and when and how the shipment should arrive.

- Express regret for the delay.

- Put in a plug for future business.

Company Name
Address
City, State Zip

Date

Mr. Russell Downing
207 Montana Avenue
Englewood, FL 33533

Dear Mr. Downing:

The BMW 325e you purchased through our European Delivery Program has arrived and is ready for pick-up. Please give me a call at 397-6622 so we can arrange a convenient time for you to come in; we are open from 9 a.m. to 6 p.m. Monday through Saturday. When you come, please bring with you a photo i.d. (driver's license) and the packet that you received from the BMW factory in Munich when you purchased the car.

I look forward to hearing from you.

Sincerely,

George H. Canfield
Customer Service

- Let the customer know what your business hours are and what he or she needs to do in order to pick up the merchandise.

Company Name
Address
City, State Zip

Date

To: Thomas B. Slocum
     42 West Oak Road
     Sherman, TX 75090

Statement for Services

March 1 - March 15

March 1
General Housecleaning 4 hrs. @ $15.00 per hr. $60.00

March 8
General Housecleaning 4 hrs. @ $15.00 per hr. $60.00

March 15
General Housecleaning 2 hrs. @ $15.00 per hr. $30.00
Yard Maintenance   2 hrs. @ $20.00 per hr. $40.00

                                        Total: $190.00

Payment is due upon receipt

- Give exact dates and hours of service.

- Specify hourly rates and total charges.

- Mention when bill is to be paid.

Company Name
Address
City, State Zip

Date

Mr. Stanley Jarvis
519 Sutton Place NW
Washington, D.C. 20027

Statement for goods delivered   April 12, 1988

Qty. 4   "Jiminy Cricket" dwarf shrubs @ $150.00 ea.

subtotal	$ 600.00
delivery charge	$ 35.00
total	$ 635.00
less deposit	$ 100.00
amount due	$ 535.00

Payment is due upon receipt.

- Note date of delivery.

- Specify, exactly, goods and quantities delivered.

- Account for all charges exactly, crediting deposits.

- Note when bill is to be paid.

Company Name
Address
City, State Zip

Date

Mr. Henry Rossbach
Skating Program Director
Perkasie Recreation Board
379 Old Hill Road
Perkasie, PA 18944

Dear Mr. Rossbach:

I would like to request the opportunity to quote for this year's ice skating show costumes. The Creative Costume Company has been making costumes for ice skating, ballet, dance, and theater productions for over fifteen years. We are known for our fast, reliable, high-quality work and reasonable prices. Our list of satisfied customers in your area includes the Cherry Hill Recreation Board Ice Show, the Doylestown Dance Troupe, and the Quakertown Thespians Company. I have enclosed pictures of some of the costumes we have made.

I would very much like to meet with you to get more information on your ice show costume requirements (approximate quantities, material, styles, etc.) so that we may submit a quote. May I see you next Thursday morning? I will call on Monday to check if this is convenient for you.

I look forward to meeting you and having the opportunity of doing business with you. Thank you.

Sincerely,

John Hathaway
Sales Manager

Enclosures

- State what you would like to quote on and why you think the customer would be interested in a quote from your company (include information about your company if the customer does not know you: brochures, samples, a client list, and testimonials are all helpful).

- Ask for the information you need to submit the quote if you don't already have it.

Company Name
Address
City, State Zip

Date

Mr. Rudyard Hamilton
3402 East 214th Street
Cleveland, OH 44117

Dear Mr. Hamilton:

It was a pleasure meeting with you last week. Thank you for your time
and for giving us the opportunity to quote on our home, automobile,
yacht, life, and disability insurance rates.

By analyzing your personal needs and financial goals, I believe we have
come up with a coverage plan that will provide you with more than
adequate protection for yourself and your family but will save you
money over your present coverage policy. I have enclosed copies of
the various proposed plans and rates.

I will call at the end of next week to see if you have any questions.

Sincerely,

Don Aggers
Account Executive

Enclosures

- Express appreciation for their time and the opportunity to present your quote.

- State what you have enclosed and highlight special features.

- Establish a time to follow up.

Company Name
Address
City, State Zip

Date

Mr. Aaron Plunkett
Odyssey Athletics
1402 Blackford Turnpike
Augusta, GA 30907

Dear Mr. Plunkett:

In response to your recent inquiry, we are pleased to submit the attached quotation for Stargazer baseball shirts, as outlined in the attached specifications. We can ship these within six weeks after we receive your order.

We sincerely appreciate your inquiry. If you need additional information, please feel free to call me at 555-3343.

Very truly yours,

Geoffrey Dungood
Sales Manager

Enclosure

- Remind the reader of his interest in your product.

- Highlight any information you may want the customer to take special notice of—for example, the delivery schedule.

- Offer to provide additional information if the customer requires it.

Company Name
Address
City, State Zip

Date

Mr. Martin Beech
32 Cricklewood Road
Milford, CT 06460

Dear Mr. Beech:

Thank you for giving Foliage Factory this opportunity to inspect your landscape plants and recommend a comprehensive treatment program. During my March 3 inspection of your property, I found black vine weevils infesting your rhododendrons. These insects are the cause of the notches on the leaves. They are a serious problem and need to be controlled as soon as possible. In addition, your maple trees have leaf spot and powdery mildew diseases, and the arborvitae have tipblight.

I recommend five treatments for your trees and shrubs annually— an application of dormant oil in the late winter in order to destroy insect eggs, followed by three treatments (one each in early spring, late spring, and summer) for continuing insect and disease control; and a late fall application of fertilizer to encourage root growth and keep the plants strong through the winter. Foliage Factory uses only the finest materials and state certified horticulturists.

Each treatment costs $33.00. There is a 10% discount if you pay for the year's five visits in advance. For your convenience, we will return each spring to continue the service unless we hear from you. You may discontinue the service at any time. If you are not pleased with the results of any treatment, let me know and I will re-treat your trees and shrubs at no extra cost. You have nothing to lose and a better landscape to gain.

If you have any questions, please call me; otherwise I will call you on Monday to set up a schedule for the treatments.

Sincerely,

Kevin MacKay

- Express appreciation for the opportunity to present your proposal.

- Say exactly what you will provide and what the customer will gain from your proposal (benefits).

- Set up a time when you will call to discuss the proposal. Don't wait for the prospect to get back to you.

Company Name
Address
City, State Zip

Date

Mr. John Bruckel
Bruckel and Associates
Fairlane Town Center
Dearborn, MI 48125

Dear John:

I'm writing to make sure that you received our proposal for your office computer system and that everything was as we had discussed over the telephone.

Do you have any questions? We have two of the units in which you were interested in stock; shall we hold them for you? I will call Monday to discuss how we might proceed.

Sincerely yours,

Sarah Wickersham
Account Manager

- Request confirmation of the proposal's receipt and offer to clarify any questions.

- Ask for a decision on the order.

- State any additional actions you have taken or intend to take.

Company Name
Address
City, State Zip

Date

Ms. Jill Bessemer
St. Mary's Hospital
1187 Wall Street
Austin, TX 78754

Dear Ms. Bessemer:

I'm enclosing our revised proposal for the printing of your admission forms (RFQ 18-9910). By changing from a four-part form to a three-part form, we can reduce the cost by $1,230.00. I have also included the second color on the first form at no additional charge.

I hope this new proposal meets your needs and your budget. We look forward to receiving your business.

Sincerely,

James Buckner
Sales Department

Enclosure

- Highlight what was changed and why.

- Solicit more feedback (if necessary).

- Ask for the order.

Company Name
Address
City, State Zip

Date

Mr. Dale Snyder
The Pine Tree Inn
45 Commodore Street
Middlebury, VT 05753

Dear Mr. Snyder:

Thank you for requesting a quote on the landscaping for the inn's renovation. We are most interested in submitting a proposal for your consideration.

Before we submit our proposal, we have a few questions that we would like you to clarify:

1. Will all the landscaping work need to be done in July, or can it be spread out over July and August?

2. Will you be supplying topsoil from elsewhere on the property, or will the contractor have to supply it?

3. Will you require all refuse trucked away, or is there a location on site that can be used as a landfill?

I will call you next Tuesday to discuss these details if I have not heard from you before then.

Sincerely,

Adam Taylor

- Express your interest.

- Make your questions as specific as possible; certainty on the details will help you make an intelligent bid.

- Set a time to follow up for the answers.

Company Name
Address
City, State Zip

Date

Mr. Keith Cockerham
Appleton Airport
1011 N. Lindale Drive
Appleton, WI 54914

Dear Mr. Cockerham:

As I told your assistant, we just received your request for quotation RFQ 1991 for the new runway lights. It must have been delayed in the mail. May we have an additional week to work on this specification? I have already faxed the specifications to the factory and am preparing a bid package for the contractors. We should be ready to review our bid with you by next Friday.

Unless I hear differently from you tomorrow, I will assume that the extension is acceptable. I will call you if the factory has any questions. Thank you for your patience and consideration.

Sincerely,

Gene Harrison
Vice President

- In an urgent matter like this, you will have phoned, but you will want the facts in writing. Send the letter by overnight service, fax, or messenger.

- Ask for a specific amount of extra time, give the reason for requesting it, and request an immediate response if your request is to be refused.

- Thank them for their understanding.

Company Name
Address
City, State Zip

Date

Mr. Trevor Fleming
Fleming Paving Co.
3029 Michigan Avenue
Indianapolis, IN 46202

Dear Mr. Fleming:

I'm confirming that we have extended the deadline for submitting bids in response to our RFQ 1993 (Parking lot paving) until 5 p.m., May 15, as we discussed on the phone this morning.

Thank you for your interest; we shall notify you of the results of the bid selection by June 10.

Sincerely,

Howard Loomis
Vice President

- State the project to which you are referring, as well as the new deadline.

- It is helpful to provide the date by which you'll be notifying them of your decision—you can cut down on the calls you'll be receiving to inquire about the decision.

Company Name
Address
City, State Zip

Date

Mr. Gary Longobucco
Concept Marketing Tools
36 Briarwood Road
Greenbrook, NJ 08812

Dear Mr. Longobucco:

Thank you for your order (PO# 10-87-C). Greentree Printers agrees to accept the special terms of net 45 days on this order, rather than our usual net 30 days, because your company will display samples of the catalog at the trade show with an appropriate credit to Greentree Printers.

We look forward to working with you on your catalog.

Sincerely,

Fran Schultz

- Identify the order and the terms that have been accepted, as well as any special conditions.

- Thank them for the business.

Company Name
Address
City, State Zip

Date

Mr. Jim Bunnell
Center Heights Shell Station
Ferry Center Road
Morgantown, WV 26505

Dear Mr. Bunnell:

I would like to confirm the price and terms of the paving of the lot for your Shell Station.

- Net price: $3,270.00

- Payment terms: 10% with order
                 40% after completion of grading
                 50% after completion of paving

I'm enclosing the invoice for the first 10%. Thank you for selecting AJ Paving. I'm sure you will be pleased with the results.

Sincerely,

Andy Jackson
President

Enclosure

- State the terms clearly.

- Indicate what you've enclosed.

- Express appreciation for the business.

Company Name
Address
City, State Zip

Date

Mr. Greg Ring
Brewer Paper Company
41 Acme Road
Brewer, ME 04412

Dear Greg:

Thank you for your order (PO #12-81-77C, #2 Boiler rebuild). We have already begun the foundation design work and expect to have prints ready for approval to you in three weeks, as promised.

There is one item open on this order: the final payment. We would like the last 25% to be paid within 30 days of completion, rather than the 45 days your financial people suggested. If this is agreeable to you, we will proceed with the acknowledgment in this fashion.

Thank you again for your order. We are looking forward to a smooth start up.

Very truly yours,

Kevin Bauer
Vice President, Sales

- Express thanks for the order.

- State what the exception is.

- State what impact the resolution of the open item has on the progress of the order.

Company Name
Address
City, State Zip

Date

Mr. James Lopez
Essex Engineering Company
75 Hickory Avenue
Forest, VA 24551

Subject: PO #18-7711-B 100HP Motor

Dear James:

Thank you for your order. Before we start engineering on this order, I just want to clarify one point. Your specification states "Class B insulation." Our standard is "Class F," which is the next higher temperature rating. It is superior to B in every way and provides you with more thermal "life" in your motor.

Unless you tell us otherwise within 10 days, we will design and build the motor with "Class F" insulation.

We very much appreciate your business.

Sincerely yours,

Roger Cook
Vice President, Sales

- Explain the changes in specification and their consequences.

- Thank the customer for his business.

Company Name
Address
City, State Zip

Date

Mr. Gary Burdette
3620 Atlanta Highway
Athens, GA 30306

Dear Mr. Burdette:

We would like to confirm the changes to the contract on Order #GMT-001762.

1. You will require the heavy-duty suspension.

2. You request the 306 V-8 engine.

3. You will pay cash and will not use our financing program.

The above changes should not affect the delivery schedule of your pickup truck. However, they will add $402.86 to the price. Your truck should be delivered in 10-12 weeks.

Thank you for choosing Athens Motors.

Sincerely,

Ed Schmidt
Sales Manager

- Detail the changes.

- Explain the consequences of the changes.

- Thank the customer for his business.

Company Name
Address
City, State Zip

Date

Mr. Ron Gratovich
Hardi Extruder Company
106 Quarry Road
Charleston, WV 25301

Dear Ron:

We would like to confirm the terms of the consignment stock of motors that we have agreed to place in your building.

1. When you draw on the consigned stock, your purchase order will trigger us to replenish the stock and invoice for the motors taken.

2. At the end of the year, a physical inventory will be taken and any adjustments will be made.

3. Either party can discontinue this agreement on two month's notice.

This program has worked very well at other companies like yours. We are looking forward to working more closely with you.

Very truly yours,

Bill MacDougall
Vice President, Sales

- Describe the ordering and billing mechanism.

- State the length of the deal.

- Thank them for their business and express optimism in the program.

Company Name
Address
City, State Zip

Date

Mr. and Mrs. Roger Lawrence
4509 Southwest 22nd Circle
Delray Beach, FL 33444

Dear Roger and Kitty:

It was so nice to see you again. I'm glad you liked the plans I proposed for the library. The soft rose color you chose for the carpet will look wonderful with the chestnut paneling and will tie in very nicely with the rest of the downstairs.

As usual, I've enclosed two copies of the contract detailing the cost of the materials (carpeting, window treatments, wallpaper, paint, and furnishings) and projected costs for the labor involved. Please sign and return one copy to me along with a check for the indicated deposit so that I may start ordering the materials as soon as possible. The other copy is for your records.

Thanks again for your business. I enjoy working with both of you very much.

Very truly yours,

Jonathan J. Monroe

Enclosures

- Indicate what is to be signed, why, and what else the client should do (e.g., return contract, send deposit).

- Express appreciation for the business.

Company Name
Address
City, State Zip

Date

Mr. Edward Ecklemeyer
Universal Electric Company
720 Stewart Avenue
Ithaca, NY 14850

Dear Ed:

Our Sales Order #GA-39482 for Universal Electric Co. (purchase order #PEC-409) requests that we transmit revised drawings for approval. The prints are enclosed with this letter; please return them by February 21. Should the prints not be returned by that date, we will have to extend the Sales Order Ship Date according to our published cycle times after the prints are returned to Athens.

Please let us know your best estimate as to when we should be receiving the approved drawings.

Thank you.

Sincerely,

Robert R. Reed
Manager, Customer Service

- Specify when the deadline is for returning the approved drawings.

- Make certain to outline the consequences of not returning the drawings on time.

Company Name
Address
City, State Zip

Date

Mr. Robert Wickersham
Wickersham Plumbers
78 Pine Street
Hayward, CA 94544

Dear Mr. Wickersham:

Because Kingsley Building Company is a prime contractor for the State of California, we are required to verify that all our subcontractors comply with the EEOC standards. Please send me a letter by April 20 stating your compliance with these standards so that we may proceed with our pending order for your supplies.

If you do not have the statement of EEOC criteria at hand, the state's regional EEOC office can send it to you.

Thank you for your cooperation.

Sincerely,

Mark Vianni
Vice President, Personnel

- State why you need to have verification of compliance and by what date you need the letter.

- If you are dealing with a business that may not have experience in this area, be helpful and guide it in the necessary direction.

Advertising and Public Relations 2

Advertising and public relations, though related in their objective of increasing acceptance of a product, service or idea, use very different approaches to reach those objectives. While public relations is frequently described as free advertising, its primary goal is to make potential buyers and clients aware of the company and products—to keep its name before the public. The primary objective of advertising is to move the buyer from awareness to purchase. In both cases, the idea is to create positive images that will attract potential customers. Both advertising and public relations must be consistent with the objectives of the business and its approach to the market in order to succeed.

Advertising. When requesting rates from print and broadcast media, be specific as to what you want and why you want it. After receiving rate information, it's always a good idea to meet with the sales person to discuss the advertising schedule and negotiate the best rates. Working with an advertising agency can sometimes be a rocky road. The letters in this section help in dealing with some of the more difficult situations.

Announcements of new businesses, branch offices, employees and such should, as a rule, be short and to the point. The challenge is to get the reader's attention, and then give him the single message you want to communicate. Brevity and focus are the keys here.

Public relations. To understand how to put together a press release, it's helpful to see what route the press release takes when it leaves your office. First, it finds its way to an editor's desk at a newspaper, magazine or broadcasting station.

The editor weeds through a pile of press releases and finds a few that look as if they would be of interest to his audience. A staff writer uses the press release as background material or rewrites the release into a story, sometimes barely changing it for the final version.

To have the best chance for publication, a press release must, therefore, be in a form that makes sense to a journalist. *Who*, *what*, *when*, *where*, *why* and *how* are the basic questions a journalist asks. Incorporate the answers to these questions in your press releases. What makes the event you are describing "newsworthy" must be clear and prominent. Be concise and accurate. And don't try to oversell your release. Journalists have a built-in baloney detector.

Company Name
Address
City, State Zip

Date

Ms. Regina Welles
The Welles Group
47 Madigan Avenue
Lisbon, OH 44432

Dear Regina:

The display ads are great. The print campaign you outlined is the best thing we've ever seen proposed. I guess we have no choice but to give you the account!

We were so excited about our meeting that we want to get this show on the road immediately. Let's get together and discuss a printer.

Next week we'll sign contracts over lunch. Call us soon to arrange the details.

So, congratulations! And thanks.

Sincerely,

Paul Blanton
Vice President, Marketing

- Simple is best. Say congratulations and tell them what happens next, and that's about it. Be upbeat and get things off on the right foot.

Company Name
Address
City, State Zip

Date

Mr. Steve Waring
The Ad Hoc Company
89 Deer Park Road
Milford, PA 18337

Dear Mr. Waring:

The Wheelhouse Discount Auto Dealership is planning a big promotion to announce the new model year, and we are interested in your agency. Please contact our Advertising Manager, Fred Tracy, to set up a meeting to discuss your fees and how you would propose to handle our account.

We want to produce two 30-second television spots and five radio spots to be aired on local stations and cable systems. We have seen some of your locally-produced commercials and were impressed with their quality and directness.

Please contact Fred as soon as possible. We want to get going with this immediately.

Sincerely,

Evan Mitchum
Advertising Director

- Tell the prospective agency what you plan to do (in general terms) and what you expect the agency to do. Your clarity will speed the process.

- Be specific about who should be contacted and when.

Company Name
Address
City, State Zip

Date

Ms. Janet Wein
The Alpha Agency
1412 Sunrise Highway
Sandusky, OH 44870

Dear Janet:

At our annual review last Friday, the Board of Directors was quite
disappointed at the soft sales growth for the last year. We have decided
to review our entire promotional effort, including our advertising
relationship with The Alpha Agency.

I'm sure you will want to be part of this review. This letter is meant to
give you an opportunity to gather some information to present your side
of the story. Please contact my office to set up a meeting.

I expect to hear from you soon.

Sincerely,

Michael Deere
Marketing Director

- This is not a pleasant task, so don't try to be too chummy. Just get to the point.

- Give them an opportunity to respond, at their initiative—but be sure they know it should be done ASAP.

Company Name
Address
City, State Zip

Date

Mr. Arthur Bonner
The Creative Partnership
23 Eaves Street
St. Louis, MO 63111

Dear Arthur:

As you know, MicroData was recently acquired by General Systems, Inc. We have found it necessary to streamline many of our operations, and all of our promotions will now be handled by the Marketing Department of the parent company in New York. We regret to inform you that MicroData will no longer be needing the services of The Creative Partnership.

We are sorry that we must end what has been a mutually beneficial relationship. Thank you again for all the work you have done for us.

Very truly yours,

R. Stanley Steele
Vice President, Marketing

- Although not all terminations will be as friendly as this, it is preferable to avoid being too negative. Try to be upbeat without being false—no need to kick them when they're down.

- If possible, conclude on a cordial note; priorities may change again in the future.

Company Name
Address
City, State Zip

Date

Ms. Julia Cavanaugh
Advertising Director
The Valhalla Register
Valhalla, NY 10595

Dear Ms. Cavanaugh:

The Quilt Barn is planning a Spring Sale, and we would like to advertise in The Register. Please send us your rate sheet, along with information about the amount of lead time The Register requires for advertisements.

If you have any special requirements for the artwork and copy to be printed, please enclose these specifications with the rate sheet.

Sincerely,

Wilma Greves

- Short and sweet. All you want is their rates and lead time (how soon before publication the ad needs to be submitted), and that's all you need to ask for.

- Cover your bases by asking if they need anything special. The chances are they don't, but you don't want to find that out too late.

Company Name
Address
City, State Zip

Date

Mr. John Bloska
Advertising Sales Manager
Business Ventures Magazine
12 Vulcan Road
Allentown, PA 18100

Dear Mr. Bloska:

We are interested in placing several advertisements in your magazine and would like to know what your rates are. Please call me or send us a rate card as soon as possible.

Our plans are to place a two-page ad in your June issue and subsequently to place a full-page ad in the next five issues. We are having the artwork done right now. If you have any special requirements for the printing of artwork, please forward those with your rate card.

We also need to know what the lead time is for the submission of ads.

If you have any questions, call me immediately.

Sincerely,

Mark Holloway
599-4328, Ext. 3

- Perhaps even more important than rates is the lead time. Magazines have a huge lead time, six months or more in some cases, so plan ahead.

- Don't forget to cover yourself by asking for their printing requirements.

Company Name
Address
City, State Zip

Date

Ms. Evelyn Wise
KING-TV
2 Battle Avenue
Seattle, WA 98101

Dear Ms. Wise:

Our company will be buying television time in August for a back-to-school shoe promotion, and we are making inquiries now to lay the groundwork. Please have a sales representative call me at 645-2300 to discuss advertising on your station.

Our preliminary plan is to run 30-second spots during the last two weeks of August. We want airtime every day during the late afternoon movie for those two weeks, and possibly during the late night movie as well, depending on how far our budget will take us.

I realize that you book these spots well in advance, and I would appreciate your immediate attention in this matter.

Sincerely,

Steve Young
Vice President, Marketing

- Broadcast advertising rates (despite rate sheets) are extremely variable, and you will probably want to negotiate them face-to-face.

- Most spots are booked months in advance, so the first thing you should do is inquire about availability and set up a meeting.

Company Name
Address
City, State Zip

To: Date:

Guilford Associates, Inc. (Guilford) hereby requests you to prepare for and on behalf of Guilford, the following:

_____
Description of Work   Date Due

Guilford agrees to pay you $ on receipt and acceptance of the work. You understand that the labor performed is a "work made for hire" and that Guilford shall own all the rights to the work in the name of Guilford or otherwise. You hereby warrant that the work will be an original work that has not been in the public domain or previously created, and that the work will be free of any unauthorized extractions from other sources. You further understand that Guilford shall have the privilege of referring to you in promotional and advertising material.

Please signify your acceptance of this agreement by completing the form below and return one copy to us at your earliest convenience.

_____
For Guilford Associates, Inc.

To: Guilford Associates, Inc.

I agree to perform the work listed above, and I accept the terms of this agreement as stated above.

_____
Signature
_____
Social Security Number
(Required by Internal Revenue Regulations)

- Your agreement should be crystal-clear as to ownership of materials produced, such as articles, artwork, or anything else created by the freelancer, and that these materials shall be original.

- Insist that freelancers sign agreements (thereby protecting you) and provide social security numbers (saving you time later).

Company Name
Address
City, State Zip

Date

Mr. Sol Linman
Linman Printing
14 Press Way
Harrison, NY 10528

Dear Sol:

Well, it finally happened. Nuevo Promos just got too big for its britches, and we had to move to a bigger office. So from now on, if you're looking for the best advertising agency since the dawn of mankind, you'll just have to go to:

Nuevo Promos
112 Atlantic Street
Stamford, CT 06906
(203) 555-4141

Call us, and we'll have Jim Prior, the account executive for your area, stop by your office to discuss your promotional needs. We will continue to offer maximum creativity at very reasonable rates.

Hope to hear from you soon.

Sincerely,

Linda Hernandez

- This letter is a fairly routine one, but do what you can to keep it from being too boring. Have fun with it and give them a reason for following up.

- Be sure the new address stands out clearly, and always include the phone number, even if it *hasn't* changed.

Company Name
Address
City, State Zip

Date

Ms. Sandra Deale
Editor
New England Video Production News
310 Charles Bank Road
Boston, MA 02113

Dear Ms. Deale:

Video Eyes—a new division of Prince Marketing—combines the creative expertise that is Prince's hallmark with a new, state-of-the-art video production facility.

The core of Video Eyes is a creative service team of independent professionals who work on projects as needed. Production managers, directors, screenwriters, computer-graphics artists and post-production specialists are all on call at the new facility.

The heart of the new subsidiary—the apple of Video Eyes—is the new post production facility. Built around a CMX edit controller, it offers full featured edit capability with list management, frame accuracy, and digital effects from a FOR A 440 TBC. Add to this full-frame graphics capability and eight-track audio mixing, and it all spells sophistication.

Sophistication is great, but more important to the video producer is configuration. All of Video Eyes capabilities are available for one remarkably reasonable rate. No add-ons, and no surprises when the bill comes. It's all right there, to be used as the production requires.

Video Eyes is located at 15 East Street, Cambridge, MA 02138. Rate sheets are available upon request.

Sincerely,

Dick Navarro
Director, Creative Group

- Treat the new subsidiary as a separate company and make sure the reader knows where to find you. Don't belabor the fact that it has been spun off from the parent. Your reader is more likely to be interested in what the subsidiary does.

- A simple mention of the parent company suggests its expertise is available to the subsidiary.

- Do some selling. Tell the reader what makes you better than everybody else.

HARVEY H. PITNEY, STEVEN P. SUPER

AND

PAUL W. GORDON

TAKE PLEASURE IN ANNOUNCING

THE FORMATION OF

PITNEY, SUPER AND GORDON

A PROFESSIONAL CORPORATION

ENGAGED IN THE GENERAL PRACTICE OF LAW

3042 CENTURY PARK
LOS ANGELES, CA 90041

(213) 554-3211

- This is a formal announcement—appropriate to professional service firms. It would not be appropriate to such businesses as a plumbing contractor or a beauty parlor.

Regional Health Care, Inc.

is pleased to announce that

Barbara Chappell, M.S.W., C.I.S.W.

has joined the firm's Santa Fe Office

as a Psychiatric Social Worker

14 Elmont Ave.
Santa Fe
638-4218

- An announcement of a new employee gets the company's name before the public and implies that your company is growing and prosperous.

From Here to Maternity

is pleased to announce

that we now offer

A COMPLETE LINE OF CHILDREN'S WEAR

INCLUDING INFANTS' SIZE 0 TO CHILDREN'S 6X

SERENDIPITY SQUARE PLAZA

6 HIGH SCHOOL AVENUE

PROVIDENCE RI

(401) 654-0234

HOURS:

MONDAY - SATURDAY 10-9
SUNDAY 12-5

Ask for Joan or Thomasina!

- Focus on your unique capabilities (here, combining two related product lines in one store).

- Give the state name and area code if you operate in an area close to the state line.

Tina's Florists

has changd its name to

BUDS, BANGLES, AND BEADS

to reflect the addition of crafts supplies...

We'll continue to serve you with all kinds of floral designs,

and, as always, we're happy to sell a single orchid

or the full arrangements for a formal wedding.

Come see us.

We're at the same address:

340 Alderman Way (Across from the Shopper's Market)
Westfield

Or give us a call at 623-0999

- Although many people suggest ads with lots of long copy, a relatively concise one like this will be less likely to dilute your points.

- If you're not sure about the design the ad should take, consult with your local paper.

Company Name
Address
City, State Zip

WILD STEVE HAS OPENED A NEW STORE IN SCOTTSDALE!

Dear Neighbor:

Central Arizona has gotten Wilder since Wild Steve opened an all new store at the Apache Mall in Scottsdale! And this store is the Wildest one yet, with 25,000 square feet of the hottest fashions at the coolest prices!

To celebrate the Grand Opening, Wild Steve is giving away free tote bags to the first 1,000 customers. So come on down and check out Wild Steve's incredible selection of women's fashion jeans for under $30, our full range of colorful tops, and Arizona's biggest collection of exercise wear!

And when you're in Phoenix or Tempe, check out our other fantastic stores.

Wild Steve's will really drive you Wild!

- Give people an incentive to use your new branch—convenience, service, selection, pricing, etc.

- Assume nothing. Pretend they've never heard of you before and remind them of what your business is all about.

- Mention your other established locations.

Company Name
Address
City, State Zip

Date

Mr. Robert McClatchey
McClatchey and Varnum
340 Windmere Road
Winnetka, IL 60093

Dear Bob:

After long consideration, Vulcan Products has decided that our public relations needs will be handled by McClatchey and Varnum. Congratulations!

We based our decision on your firm's excellent track record of dealing with mid-sized manufacturing companies. Your extensive client list, as well as the satisfaction expressed by those companies, made you the obvious choice.

As we have discussed in our preliminary meetings, Vulcan Products requires a full-service public relations approach. All inquiries not of a sales nature will be referred to McClatchey and Varnum, all of our press releases will be handled by your firm, and we will meet soon to discuss the updating and revamping of our other printed materials.

We would like to get a one-year contract signed and financial arrangements finalized as soon as possible. Please contact our legal department to work out the details and set up an appointment.

McClatchey and Varnum is an excellent firm, and we are excited about working with you. Let's hope this is the beginning of a long and profitable relationship for everyone involved.

Sincerely,

Thomas Whitehead
President

• This is a formal communication in what is probably already a dynamic relationship. Give them the good news, be sure everyone knows what's expected of them, what the next step is, and sign off.

Company Name
Address
City, State Zip

Date

Mr. Frederick Gelso
Warwick Public Relations, Inc.
109 Conch Avenue
Tampa, FL 33609

Dear Mr. Gelso:

Cableview has decided to hire a firm to handle the public relations for
our Tampa system. We are interested in your firm and would to discuss
your services and fees.

Specifically, we need a firm to handle our brochures, releases, the
annual report, and other written communications. Telephone inquiries
and letters will be handled by our Public Affairs department, which will
also coordinate our relationship with the outside public relations firm.

Please call to set up an appointment to discuss your services.

I look forward to hearing from you.

Sincerely,

Mark Obern
Executive Vice President
987-3321 Ext. 43

• Simple is best—tell them what you want and ask for the price. That's it.

Company Name
Address
City, State Zip

Date

Mr. Timothy Applebaum
News Director
WDSR-TV
1111 Main Street
Nicollet, MN 56074

Dear Mr. Applebaum:

Thank you for your invitation to be a guest on your program "Movers and Shakers." I will be at your studios at 11:00 a.m. on Tuesday, August 3 for the taping of the show.

My understanding is that the topic to be discussed is the recent acquisition of Affiliated Systems, Inc. by the Honeyman Corporation. I will represent Affiliated, Mr. James Knox will be there to give Honeyman's side of the acquisition process, and we will both be asked questions by members of the local business press who have not yet been chosen.

I have been informed that it is best not to wear a white shirt on television. If there are any other "tricks of the trade" I should know about, please contact my office. Also, if you could let me know who the interviewers will be when they are selected, I would appreciate it.

I look forward to it. See you then.

Sincerely,

Bart Willoughby

- State your acceptance, then give the time, date, and place for the interview in the first paragraph. Put any other details to be sorted out in the first paragraph.

- Be certain the topic is mutually agreed upon in writing. There is no such thing as an open-ended interview. The last thing you want is any surprises when the tape rolls.

Company Name
Address
City, State Zip

Date

FOR IMMEDIATE RELEASE

<u>Faust FX Expansion Card Adds 80386 Power to 80286 PCs</u>

The Faust EX Expansion Card is the latest addition to the Cinque Computer Products line. Built around the sophisticated 80386 microprocessor, the Faust EX combines power and speed to put any 80286 IBM-compatible computer on the cutting edge of the latest technology.

The Faust EX requires only a single expansion slot and 20 watts additional power. It can be easily installed using ordinary tools. The 80386 microprocessor can handle twice the load of a conventional 80286 microprocessor in one-quarter the time. The Faust EX comes complete with an external communications port that makes networking convenient and easy.

For more information, contact Cinque Computer Products, 207 Tarry Way, San Luis Obispo, CA 93401 (1-800-555-4567).

- *What* and *why* goes in the first paragraph as succinctly as possible. You are announcing a new product, not trying to sell it—your goal is to get the reader to remember the product name.

- *How* gets detailed in the second paragraph, along with significant features. The source of the information goes at the end.

Company Name
Address
City, State Zip

Date

FOR IMMEDIATE RELEASE

Basta Pasta Incorporated is opening its new pasta factory in Brooklyn on June 15. Soon all America will be able to savor the fresh buttery noodles and other pasta varieties from Basta Pasta.

Twenty years ago, Sal and Doris DeCiccio opened a family-style Italian restaurant in Bayside, Queens. They served the same delicious pasta that they had served to their family. It was so tasty that soon people were coming from all over the New York and New Jersey area to sample the authentic Italian taste. The DeCiccios thought "Why not make the pasta available to everyone, not just the customers at our restaurant?"

And so Basta Pasta Incorporated was born. Local residents can still get authentic Italian spaghetti, tortellini, and stuffed shells at the restaurant in Bayside. And now shoppers across the country will be able to get the pastas at their supermarkets, too!

Basta Pastas are made from only the finest ingredients—pure, golden semolina and country fresh eggs. Aside from the traditional family favorites, like manicotti and linguine, Basta Pasta also makes specialty pasta—red pepper pasta, cheese and basil pasta, even pumpkin pasta! And every box of Basta Pasta comes with a recipe for one of Doris DeCiccio's favorite pasta sauces. Now consumers can learn the secrets behind the spicy red clam sauce, or the sophisticated lemon and chicken linguine sauce.

Once your customers have tried these pastas, they'll keep coming back for more.

For wholesale orders, call our toll-free Pasta Hotline: 1-800-YO-BASTA

- Because people remember stories, it's useful to construct a narrative. Talk about why and how the business was created, and why your product or service is really necessary and/or unique.

- Be complete in discussing your product line or service. Target your audience and give them an easy way to reach you.

Company Name
Address
City, State Zip

Date

Mr. Andrew McGaffigan
Host, "Business In The News"
WNJR-AM
1210 Union Turnpike
Rahway, NJ 07065

Dear Mr. McGaffigan:

Acoustic Engineering is pleased to announce that John W. Hill will be joining the company as Special Assistant to the President. Mr. Hill will oversee new product development, as well as report directly to the President on staffing and corporate development.

Mr. Hill comes to Acoustic Engineering from the Douge Corporation, where he was Chief Engineer as well as Operations Manager of the loudspeaker division. Previously, he designed public address systems for Theatre Sounds, Inc.

Mr. Hill is a graduate of Princeton University. He lives in Manhattan with his wife, Frances, and daughter, Melanie.

Sincerely,

John Almas
President

- Begin with new position and responsibilities.

- Professional history, in the second paragraph, should include relevant items in reverse (most recent to earliest) order.

- Keep listing of personal items to a minimum.

Company Name
Address
City, State Zip

Date

FOR IMMEDIATE RELEASE

Dixie Advertising is pleased to announce that Laura Kiner has been named Vice-President, Account Supervisor. Ms. Kiner has been an Account Executive with Dixie for over five years. Her new responsibilities will include overseeing eight Account Executives as well as guiding the continued growth of Dixie Advertising. Ms. Kiner has generated accounts worth over $2.5 million in business for Dixie and has been the prime mover in the firm's recent successful campaigns for Southern Air Transport and Frontierland Amusement Park. She lives in Atlanta with her husband, Tad, and son, Tim.

- Talk about new job responsibilities first, then the previous position.

- Don't get bogged down in the specifics of the new position.

- Keep personal details to a minimum.

Company Name
Address
City, State Zip

Date

FOR IMMEDIATE RELEASE

The First Hartford Bank is proud to announce that Chief Executive Warren Hardman has been named to the Board of Directors of the United Way.

Mr. Hardman recently celebrated his twenty-third year as an employee of First Hartford. Long active in community affairs, he also sits on the board of Saint Stanislaw's Hospital and is past President of the Rotary Club of Middlesex County. Mr. Hardman feels it is a privilege to represent the Bank in such an important capacity. "I can't think of an organization that makes more of an actual difference in the community. I hope I can help them maintain that tradition."

The United Way raises money for a number of well-established charities, including the American Red Cross and The Cancer Society, through a partnership with business and community leaders.

- Keep biographical details brief and relevant to the award/achievement.

- Blow your horn, but softly.

- Include a brief explanation of the award/achievement at the end.

Company Name
Address
City, State Zip

Date

FOR IMMEDIATE RELEASE

Robert McDonald, President of McDonald Financial, Inc., and Christopher T. Martin, President of Plan-Financial, Inc., announce that their two firms will merge on November 30.

The new firm, which will be called Lifetime Financial Planning, Inc., will be located at 54 State Street, New Haven, Connecticut 06511. The telephone number is (203) 787-2982. Mr. McDonald and Mr. Martin are well-versed in financial planning, each having more than ten years of experience in the field. Mr. McDonald is a lifetime resident of the New Haven area; Mr. Martin has lived in the area since attending Yale University.

Lifetime Financial Planning is prepared to help individuals develop a financial plan at any stage in their career. The firm will specialize in aiding small-business owners and providing services to executives in local corporations.

The two firms have worked extensively with numerous local organizations and individuals. Current clients include Seth Warner, Inc., Financial Management, Inc., and Managed Plans.

- This is a typical news release—relatively low key in view of the usual overblown approach.

- Be sure to ask your clients' permission to use their names in any publicity.

Company Name
Address
City, State Zip

Date

FOR IMMEDIATE RELEASE

Edward McVay Belding has been named a partner in the law firm of Anderson & Lakewood, 150 South Ninth Street, Minneapolis, Minnesota 55428. Mr. Belding was formerly a partner of Tilson, Johns, Zapata, and Thorpe of Minneapolis. Lewis Lakewood is the senior partner of Anderson & Lakewood.

Mr. Belding is a graduate of Carleton College and the University of Michigan Law School. He served in the Marine Corps in Lebanon.

- You can go into more detail—about academic honors and job history, for example—but it's well to keep it simple. Always review copy with the person concerned, and respect his or her wishes as to what's included or left out.

Company Name
Address
City, State Zip

Date

FOR IMMEDIATE RELEASE

Martin Firearms Celebrates 70th Anniversary

Martin Firearms, a world leader in manufacturing quality pistols and rifles since 1918, is celebrating its 70th anniversary. With its headquarters located in the original factory building in Schenectady, New York, Martin Firearms employs 161 people in both corporate and manufacturing capacities. Martin Firearms is an industry leader in sportsman's rifles and supplies handguns to many police departments in the United States and Canada. Last year, over 15,000 pieces were shipped around the world. No serious gun collection is complete without a custom-made Martin Firearms hunting rifle.

- Just the facts. Try to keep it under 100 words. Tell them what you do, where you do it, how many people it takes, and what your sales are.

- Include one or two salient features if you have the room. In this case, the reader is told that this is a company whose stock in trade is quality, not volume. Although this kind of piece is primarily informational, give readers something to remember you by.

Company Name
Address
City, State Zip

Date

FOR IMMEDIATE RELEASE

Martin Firearms Celebrates 70th Anniversary

Martin Firearms, a world leader in manufacturing quality pistols and rifles, is celebrating its 70th anniversary. As part of its anniversary program, the company will conduct tours of the plant at 40 DeLong Drive in Schenectady, demonstrating all aspects of gun manufacturing, on Friday, July 11, from 10 am to 4 pm.

With its headquarters located in the original factory building in Schenectady, New York, Martin Firearms employs 161 people in both corporate and manufacturing capacities. President Preston Martin, a grandson of founder Joseph Martin, started his firearms career working summers in the tool and die shop, entered sales following his graduation from Union College in 1962, and became president in 1983.

Martin Firearms is an industry leader in sportsman's rifles and supplies handguns to many police departments in the United States and Canada. The .38 Patrol Officer's Special was adapted by the Dallas and Boulder, Colorado, police departments this year and is in use in more than 300 police departments nationwide. Last year, over 15,000 pieces were shipped around the world. No serious gun collection is complete without a custom-made Martin Firearms hunting rifle.

The company won the prestigious "Sam Houston" award six years in succession, 1981-1986, for its contribution to the sport of riflery. The award is presented each year to the rifle manufacturer who does the most to promote safety on the range.

Martin Firearms' most famous handgun was the one specially crafted and manufactured for General George Patton. The World War II officer's famed pearl-handled revolver was built to U.S. military specifications by Martin Firearms, by special order of the general. It now resides in the Smithsonian Institution in Washington.

- A longer version of a company press release is particularly well suited to local media, but can easily be edited by any publication. In it, the company can expand on the virtues of its products or services and its personnel.

- Stress recent accomplishments, sales achieved, honors won, etc.

Company Name
Address
City, State Zip

Date

Mr. George Mackie
Editor
Finance News
282 Palm Avenue
Altamonte Springs, FL 32701

Dear Mr. Mackie:

I was embarrassed to find the January copy of Finance News on my desk—since I haven't even thanked you for the great way you featured my article "CFO's Guide to the Newest Spread Sheets" in the December issue.

At least, being late gives me a chance to pass on the fact that I've had a lot of positive comments on the article.

I have two more ideas for articles, which I'll run by you as soon as they "jell."

Best wishes,

Paul Ahlstrand

- Any time you get press exposure, be sure to thank those responsible.

- Prompt thank-you's are always better, but being late is no excuse for not expressing your appreciation.

Customer Relations 3

Customer relations letters are frequently referred to as "goodwill" letters since many of them are designed to engender positive feelings on the part of the reader. But there are also letters in this category which notify customers of changes to your business, deal with meetings, appointments and payments, and one of the most sensitive issues of all, handling customers whose checks have bounced. Because it is critical to maintain the best of relations with customers, the letters in this chapter are among some of the most important a business person will ever send.

Changes in business. When announcing changes in your business—from a price increase to a new salesperson in the territory—you should present those changes in the most positive way possible. Even seemingly negative situations can provide an opportunity to stress the professionalism of your company, both in the way you handle the news and in the sensitivity shown for the customer.

Complimentary letters. While these may be among the easiest to write, beware of complimenting someone on a trivial matter. It only serves to undermine your credibility. When complimenting an individual, choose a situation that truly warrants the attention.

The fact that you've taken the time to write a personal note indicates that you're interested in the customer and puts you and your company in a good light. Do not use this type of letter to make a direct solicitation for business.

Meetings and appointments. In addition to the obvious need for covering the specific arrangements, these letters should sell you and your company. After all, the purpose of a meeting is to generate business.

Payments and returns. Letters concerning payments range from the easy "Thank you for the prompt payment" to the more difficult clarifications regarding incorrect payments, and credit/exchange policies, to no-nonsense communications regarding payment problems such as returned checks. Clarity and a rational tone are essential, for these qualities will help you to resolve problems while keeping your existing customers. After all, they are the best source for future business and for referrals to potential new customers.

Company Name
Address
City, State Zip

Date

Mr. William Trexler
Frameworks
200 Station Road
Great Neck, NY 11022

Dear Bill:

I was delighted to hear how popular our "English Manor" line of picture frames has been with your customers. We have just added a new line of Art Deco frames that appeal to customers with a similar eye for current trends. I have enclosed a brochure with color photographs of each of the ten sizes in the line, as well as measurement and component information and prices. I'm sure this line will be as big a winner for you as the "English Manor" line has been.

I'd like to be able to ship an introductory assortment of 100 frames as soon as I get a purchase order from you. Once you've looked at the photographs, you might find you prefer particular sizes. We'll be glad to put together a shipment that includes exactly the mix you want.

I'll call you early next week to discuss how you'd like to proceed.

Best regards,

Sally Potter
Sales Representative

Enclosure

- To get a current client interested in a new product, mention how much success they've been having with a product of yours they already carry.

- Be sure to include as much specific information on the new product as you can.

- Let the customer know exactly what you need to know to proceed with a first shipment and arrange to follow up on the order.

Company Name
Address
City, State Zip

Date

Mr. Chester Walker
Walker's Hardware
415 Main Street
Little Rock, AR 72203

Dear Chet:

Effective April 1, we're forced to increase the dealer's price of our "Handyman's Tool Kit" to $13.65 per unit (based on lots of 24).

For the past year we have had to pay increasingly higher prices for top-grade steel and are no longer able to absorb all of this increase ourselves. Since our goal is to continue to provide high quality tools for the avid do-it-yourselfer, we believe that the best course is to continue using this supplier. We hope you'll agree that even with the new price, the "Handyman's Tool Kit" remains an excellent value.

Best regards,

Michael Kowalski
Sales Representative

- Express regret that you have to increase prices.

- State specifically:
  - what the product now costs
  - when the increase is effective
  - why it's necessary

Company Name
Address
City, State Zip

Date

Mr. Chester Walker
Walker's Hardware
415 Main Street
Little Rock, AR 72203

Dear Chet:

I'm pleased to report that effective April 1, we'll be decreasing the dealer's price of our "Handyman's Tool Kit" to $11.75 per unit (based on lots of 24). We have signed a more favorable price contract with our high quality steel supplier and are happy to be able to pass this savings on to you.

We hope this price decrease will contribute to your continued success with the "Handyman's Tool Kit" line.

Sincerely,

Michael Kowalski
Sales Representative

- Since everyone loves to save money, be sure to bring it to the customer's attention whenever you can pass on a cost savings.

- Let them know that quality hasn't suffered even though the price is lower.

Company Name
Address
City, State Zip

Date

Ms. Patricia Loomis
PSM Office Systems
79 Wildwood Turnpike
Millburn, NJ 07041

Dear Ms. Loomis:

We have extended the hours for our copying and printing service in order to accommodate our customers' needs. We are now open from 8:00 a.m. to 9:00 p.m. Monday to Friday, 9:00 a.m. to 6:00 p.m. on Saturday, and 9:00 a.m. to 1:00 p.m. on Sunday.

We hope that you will take advantage of our longer hours soon.

Sincerely,

William Ring
Millburn Branch Manager

- Tell them what is new or different and why you've done it—to help them.

- Ask for their business.

Company Name
Address
City, State Zip

Date

RMG & Associates
185 South Broad Street
South Euclid, OH 44121

Dear RMG & Associates:

We regret we will no longer be able to accept returns for cash at Lesher
Supplies. However, we will be happy to exchange your returned goods,
with receipt attached, for credit towards any other purchase in our store.

Thank you for your understanding and for your business.

Sincerely,

Jane Noel
Manager

- Clearly outline your new policy; explain how it differs from the old policy.

- Express appreciation for their understanding/cooperation.

Company Name
Address
City, State Zip

Date

Mr. Samuel Hanson
Universal Machine Tool Co.
389 Oak Street
Paso Robles, CA 93446

Dear Mr. Hanson:

As you know, Jim Tynan has left our sales office to become an applications engineer at our head office in Chicago. Kevin Smith will be your new account manager. Kevin has worked for us for five years in our order administration department. We are pleased to have him in our office, and I'm sure he'll do an excellent job in servicing your account. To assure that the transition is smooth, I will be working with Kevin for the next two months.

I will introduce him to you on our next sales call on Thursday.

Sincerely,

Tom Trent
Sales Manager

- Give the qualifications of the new salesperson and sell him or her to your customer.

- Confirm the next meeting and assure the customer that you will help make the transition from one salesperson to another as painless as possible.

Company Name
Address
City, State Zip

Date

Dear Client:

We are pleased to advise you that we have entered into an agreement with the clearing house of Little, Ursine & Co., Inc., a long established and prestigious member of the New York Stock Exchange, to clear our customer accounts. The direct effect of this action will be that on or about May 2, your account will be carried by Little, Ursine & Co., Inc. rather than our present clearing firm, Nugent, Golden & Co.

As our clearing firm, Little, Ursine & Co., Inc. will be responsible for holding securities and cash, settling transactions, collecting dividends, issuing confirmations, and looking after the various details incidental to the clearing of accounts. In conjunction with the foregoing, the securities in your account will be insured for $2,500,000. The first $500,000 of protection, which includes up to $100,000 of protection for cash, is provided by SIPC, and the balance is provided by an insurance policy purchased by Little, Ursine & Co., Inc. from the Lolander Casualty Company.

Unless we hear from you to the contrary, your account will be delivered to Little, Ursine & Co., Inc. on or about May 2. Please call us with any questions you may have.

Very truly yours,

Michele May
Vice President, Operations

Enclosures

- Customers need to be informed of any change in administrative arrangements. Give them enough information so that they feel comfortable that everything is under control.

- Offer to answer any queries they may have—this increases the comfort level.

Company Name
Address
City, State Zip

Date

Mr. Stuart Chapman
Director, National Accounts
Loomis/Jones
200 Park Avenue
New York, NY 10010

Dear Stuart:

Congratulations on becoming Director, National Accounts. It came as no surprise to any of us here—Loomis/Jones has a widely recognized eye for sharp talent. I am sure you'll meet with the same success in New York as you did in Houston and hope that you take with you pleasant memories of your two years here in Texas.

Best regards,

Lois Simmons
Realtor

- Everyone appreciates recognition when they move up the corporate ladder. Brief, sincere congratulatory notes when customers enjoy success are important to maintaining a good client relationship.

- To avoid sounding insincere, avoid excessive detail in wishing the person success.

Company Name
Address
City, State Zip

Date

Mr. Charles Borden
Omni International Trading, Inc.
800 South Wacker Drive
Chicago, IL 60606

Dear Charlie:

Congratulations on your new position at Omni International. I was delighted to hear you'd moved into management and know Omni International will be glad they found you. I'm sure this is just the first in a long series of moves up the professional ladder.

Best of luck to you—I hope we continue to see one another at the monthly DCG luncheon.

Sincerely,

William Simpson
Manager, Customer Relations

- Take every opportunity to keep in contact with current clients. Congratulating someone on a promotion provides an ideal opportunity—it's a happy occasion, and your taking note of it shows you're alert.

- Don't be unnecessarily effusive. It's easy to step over the line between applause and flattery. For example, saying "I know you'll be President someday" exceeds the bounds of reality.

Company Name
Address
City, State Zip

Date

Dr. Kenneth Pond
Department of Nutrition and Food Science
Cornell University
Ithaca, NY 14850

Dear Ken:

I've just finished reading the article in today's issue of *The Washington Post* in which you were quoted regarding calcium deficiency in teenage girls. I've always considered you to be one of the world's experts on calcium deficiency, and I'm glad that a respected newspaper such as *The Washington Post* agrees with me.

I hope you are well. I expect to be going to Ithaca later this spring; if so, I'll be sure to call you so we can get together. I'm currently working on marketing orange juice with added calcium for my company, and I'd like to discuss a couple of ideas with you.

Congratulations again on being quoted in such a prestigious source.

Best wishes,

Harlan D. Jones

- Indicate where you read or heard the quote.

- Tie the event or issue in with your own business affairs if feasible—don't force it.

Company Name
Address
City, State Zip

Date

Mr. Horace M. Long
H. M. Long and Company
54 Pine Street
West Lebanon, NH 03784

Dear Horace:

Thank you for inviting me to your open house. It was a wonderful party, and I enjoyed meeting your associates very much.

Congratulations on your beautiful new office. The view you have of the river is spectacular, and I like the way you've redesigned the interior, especially how you've opened up the roof to let in more light. It's hard to believe that place was once a hat factory!

I wish you all the best in your new location.

Sincerely,

Jim Fuller

- Include your wish for their business success in the new office.

- Be as specific as possible, especially with customized designs that the tenant will be particularly proud of.

Company Name
Address
City, State Zip

Date

Mr. Larry Lobeck
Manager
Tamale Towers
1489 Federal Road
Houston, TX 77005

Dear Larry:

On my sales call to your restaurant last week, I noticed that you were breaking ground for an addition. Congratulations on the expansion of your business.

Please let me know if I can be of any help in meeting your increasing needs for Tres Equis Beer. I look forward to working with you in serving your additional customers.

Sincerely,

Paul Logan

- Compliment the owner or manager on the obvious success of the business.

- Express an interest in serving the additional business, if appropriate.

Company Name
Address
City, State Zip

Date

Dr. Peter Rowe
Cleveland Clinic
3908 Euclid Avenue
Cleveland, OH 44110

Dear Dr. Rowe:

I very much enjoyed your article about the value of "orphan drugs" in the Sunday, March 15 edition of *The Plain Dealer.* I completely agree with you that our society will be in trouble unless something is done to stimulate the continued production of these drugs.

I am a distributor of one of these drugs, TRX-94, and I would like very much to speak with you about some of the points you discussed. I'll call you next week to see if we can arrange a convenient time to meet.

Sincerely,

Warren K. Hamlish

- State where you read the article and what you enjoyed about it.

- Make clear your connection with the topic, especially if you anticipate further contact. You want the letter's recipient to think about your interests before such contact.

Company Name
Address
City, State Zip

Date

Mr. George Unger
35 Peter Street
Newton, MA 02158

Dear Mr. Unger:

Thank you for your letter suggesting that we have a pick-up and delivery service for our dry cleaning stores. I think it's a good idea, and my partners and I will be looking into the feasibility of having such a service.

We at Hawley Dry Cleaning are always looking for ways to improve our services to our customers.

We appreciate your taking the time to write us. Thank you for your continued patronage of our stores.

Sincerely,

Robert J. Hawley
Manager

- Express appreciation for any suggestion that a customer thinks will improve your business.

- If you have taken action due to the suggestion, state what you've done.

- Express thanks for their being a customer.

Company Name
Address
City, State Zip

Date

Mr. John G. Farmer
15 Bermuda Street Wharf
New Orleans, LA 70117

Dear Mr. Farmer:

Thank you for writing and letting us know how much you enjoyed staying at Cypress House during your recent visit to Charleston. My wife, Betty, and I both take great pride in the restorations we have made to Cypress House; we are happy that our guests enjoy what we have done.

I'm enclosing the recipe for She-Crab Soup that you requested. Jim Tate, our chef, was delighted when I relayed to him how much you enjoyed the soup.

It was a pleasure having you here with us, and all of us at Cypress House hope that you'll visit us again in the near future.

Best wishes,

Sam deWinter

Enclosure

• Express appreciation for the business, as well as the compliment, and ask for continued patronage.

• Make the reply as personal as possible and show that you have valued the compliment enough to relay it to those responsible in your business.

Company Name
Address
City, State Zip

Date

Mr. George Poole
Director of Human Resources
Robomatix, Inc.
100 Renaissance Plaza
Detroit, MI 48226

Dear George:

It was a pleasure catching up with you on Thursday and hearing that Robomatix wants to proceed with training for mid-level managers. I'm sure we can put together a program that is every bit as successful as the one we did for your support staff last year.

I believe we could proceed most quickly and productively if you, Marty, Gene, and I got together for a few hours one day next week to discuss program development, scheduling, and costs. By then I'll have developed a few possible program formats that can serve as the basis for our discussion about just what type of program best meets the company's objectives.

Either Tuesday, Wednesday, or Thursday of next week is fine for me—I'll leave it up to you, Gene, and Marty to choose a date and time that is most convenient for you. I'll call you on Friday after you've had a chance to check your schedules.

I look forward to seeing you again soon.

Best regards,

Howard Stamp
President

- Be sure to mention what you hope to accomplish at the meeting (informal agenda) as well as who should be there.

- Show willingness and flexibility to work within others' schedules.

- Set a time to confirm plans.

Company Name
Address
City, State Zip

Date

Mr. George Poole
Director of Human Resources
Robomatix, Inc.
800 South Wacker Drive
Chicago, IL 60606

Dear George:

I'm glad you, Gene, and Marty all have time available next Tuesday morning, May 8, to discuss the program for mid-level managers. I'll be at your office at 10 so we'll have a few minutes to review the formats I've developed before we all meet at 10:30.

I'm planning to bring a few overheads with me to give you all an idea of the teaching materials I've found particularly effective with groups like yours. Can we arrange for a small conference room with an overhead projector?

I look forward to seeing you again and to moving ahead with plans when we meet next week. Thanks for making it all happen.

Best regards,

Howard Stamp
President

- State the date, time, and location of your meeting.

- Mention any equipment you need and why you need it.

- Express appreciation to the person who set up the meeting.

Company Name
Address
City, State Zip

Date

Mr. John Gates
HiTech Office Systems
500 Saratoga Road
Gastonia, NC 28052

Dear Mr. Gates:

Thank you for choosing NC Advertising for your expansion campaign.
We look forward to working with you in making the next year the best in
HiTech's history.

May I bring along my associate, Pauline Green, when we meet on
Wednesday, April 25? Pauline is our expert on promoting service
businesses, and she'll be able to highlight the areas your company
should emphasize in your promotions.

Sincerely,

Martin Michaels
Account Supervisor

- Give a reason why your associate will be an asset at the meeting.

- Touting an associate's or subordinate's expertise enhances the image you project,
  demonstrating your security and self-confidence in your own position.

Company Name
Address
City, State Zip

Date

Miss Robin Waite
The Stork's Store
7754 West 97th Place
Overland Park, KS 66204

Dear Miss Waite:

It was a pleasure speaking with you on the phone last week. Thank you for your interest in Daisy Diaper Covers. It's always cheering to find people who care about the ecology and want to avoid disposable diapers. We are the revolutionary alternative to diaper pins and rubber pants. As our enclosed brochure explains, our patented design allows air to circulate but won't let wetness pass through, so clothes are kept dry while heat does not build up in the diapers, reducing the chance of diaper rash. Our velcro fasteners make changes easy and eliminate sharp pins.

I will be in your area the week of April 15. May I stop by at 2:30 p.m. on Wednesday, April 17, to show you some of our samples and answer any questions you may have about our diaper covers? I will call next week to confirm with you that this time is convenient for you. I look forward to meeting you.

Sincerely,

Mike Parris
Sales Representative

Enclosure

- Be specific as to the time, date, place, and purpose of the appointment.

- Set up a time to confirm the appointment.

Company Name
Address
City, State Zip

Date

Mr. and Mrs. John Spangler
2740 Duhallow Way
South San Francisco, CA 94080

Dear Cynthia and John:

Thank you for calling and letting me know that you're interested in putting your condominium on the market. I would be very pleased to represent you in this sale. I look forward to coming over to appraise your place and to providing you with a comparative market analysis. I'll also discuss with you how I can help you get the best possible exposure and the best possible price for your property.

As we agreed over the phone, I'll be at your condominium next Thursday at 2:00 p.m.

Very truly yours,

Helen R. Hoffman

• State the date, time, and place of the appointment, as well as what you hope to achieve.

Company Name
Address
City, State Zip

Date

Mr. Michael Preston
North Communications
670 White Way
St. Paul, MN 55404

Dear Mike:

It was a pleasure meeting with you last Friday. Thank you for letting me show you how Coleman Productions can handle all your program needs and improve your video productions.

I'm enclosing the literature that you requested on our computer graphics and animation services along with a copy of our demo tape, which I thought you'd find interesting. I will call you next week to see whether you have any questions. I look forward to exploring the possibilities of our working together.

Sincerely yours,

Wilfred I. Binstock

Enclosures

- Follow up on what occurred during the meeting (e.g., request for more information) in order to get more contact if your aim is to solicit business.

- Be assertive but don't act, particularly early in a relationship, as if doing business is a certainty.

Company Name
Address
City, State Zip

Date

Mr. Conrad Stephens
CS Electronics
4892 Vista Way
Phoenix, AZ 85016

Dear Mr. Stephens:

Thanks for all your help setting up my appearance at the regional
business development meeting today. I feel that it went very well and
that you deserve a great deal of the credit.

I have one favor to ask. Is it possible for someone to send me a list of
the people who attended the meeting? I generally create a seating
chart so I can link names and faces, but unfortunately I had no time to
do that. If it's easier, just jot the names at the bottom of this letter and
return it to me. Again, thank you very much.

Best wishes,

Barry O'Connor

- Get the thank-you up front and reinforce it at the end.

- Since names are all important in sales (in life?), asking for a list of attendees is perfectly
  appropriate (and essential for follow-ups).

- Asking the reader to reply by writing on the letter itself makes a prompt response likely.

Company Name
Address
City, State Zip

Date

Mr. Kyle Taylor
The Warren Group
708 Worth Avenue
Palm Beach, FL 33480

Dear Kyle:

I'm sorry I missed our meeting last Tuesday. As I explained to your secretary over the phone, all flights out of Boston on Monday and Tuesday were canceled due to the snow storm we had. I'm glad my colleagues from Atlanta were there to present our proposal to you. I have already spoken with them, and they have briefed me on the concerns you expressed during the meeting about the scheduled delivery dates. I'm researching that right now, and I'll call you on Monday with some answers.

I would also like to schedule another meeting with you before the end of March. Is the morning of March 26 convenient for you?

Sincerely,

Tim Bournehoft
Sales Engineer

- Explain why you missed the meeting.

- If the meeting went on as scheduled without you, get information as to what went on and what your responsiblities, if any, are.

- Schedule another meeting if necessary.

Company Name
Address
City, State Zip

Date

Mr. Dwayne Newall
City Life Insurance, Room 1550
43 Madison Avenue
New York, NY 10010

Dear Dwayne:

Please forgive me for missing our lunch Tuesday. My problem was an overturned tractor trailor on I-95. You may have heard about it on the news. Had I been near an exit, I might have had a shot at it, but as it was, I sat in my car for close to two hours.

Then, when I finally got to New York, I heard you had already left for your cruise. I hope that you'll forgive me and that we can try to meet again when you return.

Best wishes,

Barbara Jackson

- Apologies are best delivered on the phone or in person. In this case, that obviously wasn't possible. Next best is a hand-written note on personal stationery. For a business associate, company letterhead is also an alternative.

Company Name
Address
City, State Zip

Date

Ms. Linda Jackson
32 Seymour Road
Atlanta, GA 30344

Dear Ms. Jackson:

I've enclosed your check for #325 for $532.23, which was returned by your bank because of "insufficient funds." Because I'm sure this problem is the result of an oversight or some mistake on the bank's part, please call me at 655-3241 and tell me how to proceed.

Sincerely,

Carlos Erickson
Vice President

Enclosure

- People are funny about having their honesty called into question. If you have a long-standing relationship with the customer and there is no history of previous problems, a polite letter like this one will get the results you want.

Company Name
Address
City, State Zip

Date

Ms. Linda Jackson
32 Seymour Road
Atlanta, GA 30344

Dear Ms. Jackson:

On April 4, we redeposited your check #325 for $532.23, as you requested in our April 3 phone conversation, and it has again been returned to us marked "insufficient funds." We are sure this is as embarrassing for you as it is frustrating for us, but we must insist that you call us immediately and make arrangements to pay your bill by money order or cashier's check so that we may keep your account current.

Sincerely,

Carlos Erickson
Vice President

- Switching from "I" to "We" (meaning the firm) makes this letter sound sterner.

- A check that has been returned a second time is a signal that your once-solid customer may be having financial difficulties. But if he or she pays up at this point you may want to forget the matter.

Company Name
Address
City, State Zip

Date

Ms. Linda Jackson
32 Seymour Road
Atlanta, GA 30344

Dear Ms. Jackson:

We have not heard from you since your check (#325) for $532.23 was returned by your bank a second time. If we do not receive payment within seven days, we will have to place your account with a collection agency, with all the unpleasantness (and damage to your credit rating) that this implies.

Sincerely,

Carlos Erickson
Vice President

- Transferring an account to a collection agency will assure that you've lost your customer, so you should provide the customer with one more chance to pay before doing so.

Company Name
Address
City, State Zip

Date

Ms. Lynn Pearl
320 Pipers Lane
Columbus, OH 43228

Dear Ms. Pearl:

On May 10, we received your payment of $95.00 for April lawnmowing and weeding services. We have noticed that in the year you've been our customer, you have paid well in advance of the 15th every single month. We'd like to reward your promptness—this kind of payment schedule is an immeasurable help in running our business.

Starting with this month, we'll deduct 2% from your monthly bill each time you pay by the 15th.

Thank you again for your patronage.

Best wishes,

Glen Hansen
President

- Reliable, loyal customers should be rewarded. A simple "thank you" might have been enough in this case, but issuing a small discount packs more of a wallop.

- In small firms, the president should sign the letter.

Company Name
Address
City, State Zip

Date

Ms. Maddie Ford
543 Abner Doubleday Way
Gaithersburg, MD 20760

Dear Ms. Ford:

Thank you for your payment of $73.95 for your recent order of swimming pool supplies. You might like to know more about our swimming pool maintenance contract, which spares you the task of carrying heavy containers of chlorine and algacide and ensures that your pool is at all times clean and safe. In your area, a pool maintenance contract usually includes a twice-monthly visit by one of our professional service people as well as all necessary supplies. The actual cost varies depending on the size and location of your pool, but it is usually about the same expense as performing the work yourself.

Mr. John Hardy, the professional responsible for your area, will be maintaining the pool of one of your neighbors next week, and he will call you to see if you would like a free estimate.

Sincerely,

Kyle Lapham
President

- Try to interest the customer by filling a need—in this case, one implied by the need to carry heavy containers of pool cleaning supplies.

- If you promise someone will call, set up some system to ensure that they actually do so.

Company Name
Address
City, State Zip

Date

Ms. Cassie Tate
Tables by Tate
18D Beach Road
Melbourne, FL 32951

Dear Ms. Tate:

Enclosed are the table linens you ordered on April 10 and our invoice
#MFL-4X09 for $898.37. Please note that if we receive payment within
10 days, you may discount the invoice by 4%. This discount is double
our usual 2% discount and is available only during this quarter, so I urge
you to take advantage of it.

We hope you enjoy the linens and that you will call us with another
order soon.

Yours very truly,

Sandra Lockwood

Enclosure

- Offer a special discount for early payment when cash flow is a concern.

- Let the customer know right away what he/she did to qualify for the discount—stating your
time requirement exactly.

- Urge the customer to take advantage of the opportunity.

Company Name
Address
City, State Zip

Date

Mr. Harold Bloom
Asheville Park Towers, Apt. 7
700 Biltmore Avenue
Asheville, NC 28803

Dear Mr. Bloom:

Today we received your payment of $550.00 for catering services we performed at your Christmas party. Unfortunately, this is the third time you have paid for our catering services more than 60 days after the date of the invoice, despite our stated policy of payment within 10 days. As you can understand, a small business like ours must pay close attention to cash flow. Our suppliers demand cash up front, and we must have sufficient cash on hand to pay them.

In the future, we'll have to require that you pay for our catering services in advance. After a year, we'll be glad to reconsider our position since you have been a good customer in the past.

Sincerely,

Kerry Wolfe
President

- All the reasons given in the letter are valid—small businesses live and die on cash flow. You may lose this customer—but you probably can't afford to keep him on this basis.

- You'll notice there's no—"please call me if you have any questions" in this letter. You want to sound (and be) firm.

Company Name
Address
City, State Zip

Date

Mr. J. B. Boone
Cape May Pools
236 Justine Avenue
Houma, LA 70360

Dear Mr. Boone:

We have received your check #9749 for $1,610.24 in payment of our
May statement. Although our statement showed shipping charges,
Cape May was entitled to deduct this cost ($77.24) because the
statement was paid within seven days. We have credited your account
for these charges, and the credit will be reflected on your June
statement.

If you have any questions, or if we can be of further service, please call
us at the telephone number below.

Sincerely,

Bernard Holt
555-2900, ext. 37

- Customers delight in being told that they're due money, and it reflects well on the supplier if you notice the error and credit the customer promptly.

- Avoid making the customer feel that he or she made a stupid mistake.

Company Name
Address
City, State Zip

Date

Ms. Margot Robertson
150 North Pine Street
Branford, CT 06405

Dear Ms. Robertson:

We received your check #540 for $48.00 for our driveway plowing last month. I think you must have overlooked the usual surcharge of $12 for plowing after the second storm, when the snowfall exceeded 8 inches.

There's no need to pay us separately for the surcharge; we will add it to SnowBusters' next monthly statement.

Thank you for your patronage.

Sincerely,

Bryce R. Goodhue

Attachment

- Even if an unpaid item was clearly stated on an invoice, assume an inadvertent oversight if dealing with a regular customer. (People sometimes don't read statements carefully.)

- Reminding a customer of your reasonable attitude reflects well on your company and will build good will.

Company Name
Address
City, State Zip

Date

Mercury Video Deliveries
200 North Michigan Avenue
Chicago, IL 60611

Dear Accounts Payable Supervisor:

We have received your payment of $198.54 (check #2361) for our invoice #002189. Unfortunately, you have a balance due of $12.30 because you have overlooked the relevant tax and freight charges.

Please send your check as soon as possible so that we can stop the computer's collection letter sequence, which most people find extremely annoying.

Very truly yours,

Robin Johnson
Collection Supervisor

- It's better to have a person's name, even for form letters, but this salutation is better than "Gentlemen."

- Be sure to include all relevant information: amount paid, check number, and invoice number.

- The ending sentence humanizes the "form" letter.

Company Name
Address
City, State Zip

Date

Mr. Dorman F. Hillhouse, CPA, P.C.
600 Skiff Street
Baltimore, MD 21213

Dear Mr. Hillhouse:

Enclosed is our check #2032 for $212.50. You apparently paid your
June bill for computer services twice, resulting in an overpayment of that
amount. Ordinarily, we would give you a credit, but since you have
plans to close the office for the months of July and August, we believe
you would prefer to have a check.

Have a good vacation.

Best wishes,

Chris J. Risch

Enclosure

- Most customers do not object to receiving a credit. You must provide a check if the customer requests one, however.

- In this case, the writer knows the customer personally, so wishing him a good holiday is totally appropriate.

Company Name
Address
City, State Zip

Date

Mrs. Helen Stargis
14 Oak Terrace
Rutland, VT 05701

Dear Mrs. Stargis:

As requested, here is a copy of our invoice #2160543 for the merchandise we shipped to you on March 17. I've also enclosed a copy of our newest catalog; we welcome your next order and hope that you will call us whenever we can help you.

Yours very truly,

Warren Palmer
Billing Department

Enclosure

- Refer to the invoice enclosed by number and note the date of shipment.

- Take advantage of every opportunity to interest your customer in another sale. You might consider adding a handwritten "P.S." referring to a specific product. Research shows that the "P.S." gets read first.

Company Name
Address
City, State Zip

Date

Mr. Tony Walters
420 Lakeland Boulevard
Kokomo, IN 46901

Dear Mr. Walters:

We received your return of the model 42Z11 Zip-o-mat power saw
(invoice #120211) and are happy to exchange it for model 51X12, which
we hope is more suitable to your needs. Since model 51X12 is priced
lower than model 42Z11 (at $89.95), we have credited your account
$20.00.

I've enclosed a copy of our new spring catalog in which we feature a
new line of small handheld power tools that appeals to home woodworking enthusiasts like yourself. Please call at 1-800-246-6660 or use
the form in the catalog whenever you would like to place another order.

Sincerely,

Donald VanHoff

Enclosure

- Show you're truly interested in seeing that the customer gets what he or she needs.

- Refer specifically to the model ordered, shipping invoice, and amounts billed. State how
  under or overpayment will be handled (i.e., we credited your account).

Company Name
Address
City, State Zip

Date

Mr. Eugene Jarvis
10 Polk Place
Lorton, VA 22416

Dear Mr. Jarvis:

We are sorry to hear the model 1240G Deluxe Router we shipped you
on March 4 (invoice #22610) did not fulfill your expectations and are
happy to credit your account $129.98 for its return.

I've enclosed a copy of our new spring catalog. We feature a complete
line of power tools designed specifically for the home woodworker.
Please use this catalog's order form or call us at 1-800-246-6660
whenever we can help you with another order.

Sincerely,

Donald VanHoff

Enclosure

- Express regret that your product didn't satisfy the customer.

- Take every opportunity to get the customer interested in other products.

Acknowledgment of Refund for Damaged Goods (3-39)

Company Name
Address
City, State Zip

Date

Mr. Clint LaPointe
154 Bormann Road
Cazenovia, NY 13035

Dear Mr. LaPointe:

We're sorry the model 182CZ handdrill you ordered (invoice #26675) did not arrive safely and are happy to refund your $62.95 (enclosed check #8669). Unfortunately, we have no more model 182CZ drills in stock, since we discontinued the line this spring.

Here is a copy of our new summer catalog, which features a complete line of tools for the home woodworker. Model 184CZ (p. 22) is closest in price and speed to the 182CZ. We hope you will consider ordering the 184CZ, which has two more drill bits than the older model.

We apologize for any inconvenience you suffered and hope we will have another opportunity to ship you one of our fine products.

Sincerely,

Donald VanHoff

Enclosure

- Express sincere apologies for any customer dissatisfaction.

- Refer specifically to order, invoice, and check numbers and amounts.

- Show interest in continuing the customer relationship by suggesting other suitable products.

Company Name
Address
City, State Zip

Date

Ms. Deborah Bovan
Designer Depot Company
25 Green Road
Shaker Heights, OH 44122

Dear Ms. Bovan:

I'm glad you called to check on the status of the 25 sweaters you sent back to us two weeks ago. After checking our records carefully, I find that we have not received your returned sweaters. Please contact your shipper to start tracing the shipment. I'm sorry, but we cannot be responsible for returned goods that are lost in transit. However, if you send me the details in writing (sales order number, shipping company name, shipment number, date it was shipped, etc.), I will gladly help you trace it from this end.

Please keep me posted. We value your business and look forward to assisting you whenever possible.

Sincerely,

Sean McIntyre

- Be clear as to who will be responsible if the returned goods are not located.

- Express interest in resolving the matter and in helping when possible.

Handling Customer Complaints 4

There are no complaint-free businesses. In fact, dissatisfied customers who silently take business elsewhere are a far worse problem than those who complain. A customer who complains can usually be salvaged. Businesses should take the time to solicit feedback from their customers, especially unhappy ones.

Ideally, complaints should be handled on the phone. A customer's complaint can best be understood in a conversation. If the customer cannot be reached, or a discussion doesn't resolve the situation, a letter is required. In any case, a letter confirming the details of the conversation should be sent.

Whether the customer's complaint has any basis or not, the letter writer needs to acknowledge in some way that the company welcomes hearing from the customer for any reason. Even seemingly frivolous complaints can reveal significant needs for improvement in customer relations. The tone of the letter should reflect the fact that company people are approachable and ready to help if possible.

Justified complaints. If the complaint is justified, the company should respond immediately, offering to "make things right" if possible, or offering alternative solutions if that's not possible. The tone should not be defensive or cringing. After all, mistakes happen, even in the best run company. If the company has made an error, admit it promptly and make amends as best you can. Because customers are so accustomed to shabby treatment, promptness in satisfying them may even make them into public relations people for your firm. They may comment to others on the company's unusual responsiveness.

Partially justified complaints. The key here is in the approach you take. Focus on the fact that the customer is partially right. Ignore the fact that this also makes him or her partially wrong. It's far harder to get a new customer than to keep the good will of an old customer. If there's any element of truth in what the customer is saying, it is better to agree (and make things right, even if it costs money) than it is to get into a no-win argument. Similarly, in cases of misunderstanding, the thrust is for the company to take at least part of the responsibility (a miscommunication has two possible causes—a garbled message or an inattentive receiver.)

Unjustified complaints. If you believe the customer is unjustified, ask for clarification—it may be that he has not expressed himself well and the complaint is the result of a simple misunderstanding that can be easily cleared up. If you are unable to respond positively, an honest, straightforward "no," along with the reasons for the refusal, is best. If the company is not responsible, suggest the action the customer can take to get satisfaction elsewhere, without actually blaming someone else. It's unlikely the customer is trying to cheat the company, and accusing him of that will ensure undying enmity. This type of ill will can spread to other customers of your company.

To sum up, respond positively and promptly to all complaints—and consider even the most vituperative attack as providing valuable information about customer relations.

Company Name
Address
City, State Zip

Date

Mr. Frank Delaplaine
830 N. Carrollton Avenue
Baltimore, MD 21217

Dear Mr. Delaplaine:

Here's the breakdown that you requested of the billing on your sound system (PO #88177-B, Factory Order 96N-00182):

Suborder	Description	Amount
1GA	amplifier	$ 106.24
2GA	turntable	$ 261.89
3GA	speakers	$ 649.41
	Subtotal:	$ 1,017.54
	State tax (5%):	$ 50.88
	Freight:	$ 17.50
	Total:	$ 1,085.92

I hope this will allow you to pay the invoice. If you have any further questions, please call me at 889-6249.

Respectfully yours,

James Conklin

- Be clear—show all discounts, taxes, freight, etc.

- State your expectations—that the customer will either pay the invoice or call.

Company Name
Address
City, State Zip

Date

Mr. Bruce Feinstein
35 Main Street
South Hadley, MA 01075

Dear Mr. Feinstein:

I would like to apologize for the error we made on our invoice DCI-92J, dated June 15. I'm canceling that invoice and reinvoicing you as follows:

12	tables @ $11.48 each	$137.76
48	chairs @ $2.05 each	98.40
12	tablecloths @ $1.88 each	22.56
24	5-piece place settings @ $3.24 each	77.76
	Subtotal	$336.48
	Tax (4.5%)	15.14
	Total	$351.62

I hope this resolves the issue to your satisfaction. I look forward to doing more business with you in the future.

Sincerely,

Bill Simmons

- Explain what action you will take (reinvoice, credit, accept deduction, etc.)

- Solicit more business.

Company Name
Address
City, State Zip

Date

Mr. Robert J. Hudak
45 Yankee Peddler Path
Madison, CT 06443

Dear Mr. Hudak:

Thank you for calling last week regarding our error in your billing last
month. Your check (#489) was credited to the wrong account due to an
error in our computer records. I have corrected the situation, and I'm
very sorry for the inconvenience that our error has caused.

Please take a moment to review our records and confirm that we now
have your information correctly in our computer:

Cardholder:	Robert J. Hudak
Address:	45 Yankee Peddler Path
	Madison, CT 06443
Home phone:	(203) 245-4872
Work phone:	(203) 266-6079
Account number:	128-9771-553

Thank you for your understanding. We look forward to serving you in
the future.

Sincerely,

Bill Salvatore
Credit Manager

- Apologize for the error.

- State the action you took or to be taken by another party (e.g., submit corrected information).

- Confirm the correctness of your present records.

Company Name
Address
City, State Zip

Date

Mr. Hasan Kebebian
Kebebian Rugs, Inc.
578 Broad Street
Lorton, VA 22079

Dear Mr. Kebebian:

I'm sorry that we have not been able to deliver as scheduled your shipment of rugs from India. Unfortunately, the dock workers' strike in New York has prevented the unloading of the ship. I expect that the strike will be over soon and that we can deliver your shipment within the next month.

I apologize for the delay and inconvenience this has caused you. I will notify you as soon the strike is over.

Very truly yours,

Jim Castalucci
Customer Service Representative

- Explain the reason for the delay.

- Give your best estimate of reschedule.

- Express empathy, whether the delay is caused by you or by others.

Company Name
Address
City, State Zip

Date

Mr. Stan Walton
15 Federal Road
Hemlock, NY 14466

Dear Mr. Walton:

I'm sorry we sent you the Mahogany Queen Anne Footstool Kit (No. 347A) instead of the Cherry Queen Anne Footstool Kit (No. 347B) that you ordered. I am sending you the correct kit today. Please return the mahogany kit to us by UPS with insurance; we will reimburse you for all shipping costs.

Again, I apologize for the inconvenience this has caused you. Thank you for your help and understanding. We truly appreciate your business and look forward to serving you again in the near future.

Sincerely,

Jason Fine
Customer Service

- Acknowledge the error and express your apology.

- Say what you have done and/or what the customer should do to corrrect the error.

Company Name
Address
City, State Zip

Date

Mr. David Young
38 Petrified Tree Pass
Billings, MT 59101

Dear Mr. Young:

I'm sorry to learn about the damage to the sofa that you purchased from us last month. Our driver has determined that the damage occurred in shipment (most likely from the manufacturer's warehouse to our store).

I've ordered an exact replacement from the factory, and I've been told that it will take four to six weeks to get here. I'll call you as soon as it arrives, and we will arrange a convenient time for delivery.

I am very sorry for the inconvenience this has caused you. I'll be in touch very soon.

Sincerely,

Bob Chamberlain
Manager

- Acknowledge the party responsible for the damage.

- Outline corrective action taken or to be taken.

- Make sure that you follow up as promised.

Company Name
Address
City, State Zip

Date

Mrs. Lucille Jackson
1150 Oriole Street
Baltimore, MD 21217

Dear Mrs. Jackson:

Please accept my sincerest apologies for the rudeness you experienced at our restaurant last night. There was no excuse for the way you were treated, and the person involved is no longer employed at PJ Willy's. PJ Willy's prides itself on being a family restaurant where good food and good service are always "on the menu."

I hope that you will try us again. Please call me at 459-3398, and I will be very happy to take your reservations for a dinner for two on the house. Thank you for your understanding and for bringing this matter to my attention.

Very truly yours,

Bill Robinson
General Manager

- Acknowledge and apologize for the rudeness.

- Outline the corrective action to be taken.

- Ask the customer to try you again and offer an incentive (a free dinner) for doing so.

Company Name
Address
City, State Zip

Date

Mr. Patrick Blakely
964 Monroe Avenue
Malden, MA 02148

Dear Mr. Blakely:

I am sorry that the instruction manual for operating your new Frostee-Lite ice cream maker was missing. I am sending you a new manual along with a booklet of recipes for some wonderful ice cream and sherbet delights that you might like to try.

Thank you for your understanding and for selecting Frostee-Lite. I'm sure you will be very pleased with your new ice cream maker.

Sincerely,

Jana Rossman
Customer Service

Enclosure

- Apologize for the missing documentation.

- Enclose the missing documentation.

- Express appreciation for the business.

Company Name
Address
City, State Zip

Date

Mr. Sal Marino
Fast Start Automotive Products
30 Broad Street
Milford, CT 06460

Dear Mr. Marino:

We're sorry to learn of the damage to our latest solenoid shipment (PO# 77J-4P). You should file a damage claim with the trucking firm, as our standard terms and conditions of sale state "FOB factory." Our responsibility therefore ends when the trucker signs for the shipment. I have enclosed a copy of the trucker's pick-up slip, showing that the shipment was in good condition, in case this will help you in filing a claim.

We have enough stock on hand to reship your order. If you would like us to do so, please call us with a purchase order.

Sincerely,

John Bloom
Customer Service Manager

Enclosure

- State clearly who is and who is not responsible.

- Be as helpful as possible to the customer.

- Express empathy.

Company Name
Address
City, State Zip

Date

Mr. George G. Mallion
The Computer Science Corporation
66 Geese Lake Drive
Oberlin, OH 44074

Dear Mr. Mallion:

Thank you for writing us about your irritation concerning the delay in CSC's receipt of four (4) MacDonald Customized Video Display Terminals (CSC PO# 3214; our invoice #80-1219-G).

The delay, however, was not caused at our end. As specified in your Purchase Order, we shipped via Transcontinental Truckers before July 14. The terminals were actually picked up on July 12, as you can see from the enclosed copy of the bill of lading (Transcontinental #55-MC-9906).

Unless I have misunderstood something, it appears that Transcontinental is responsible for the delay. Please let me know if I may help further in this matter.

Sincerely,

James B. MacDonald
Enclosure

- Acknowledge the customer's complaint. Reference all purchase orders, invoices, etc.

- Be direct about where the fault (if any) lies.

- Appear flexible; there may be additional issues the customer will raise subsequently.

Company Name
Address
City, State Zip

Date

Miss Estelle deWinter
380 Orion Circle
Palm Beach, FL 33480

Dear Miss deWinter:

I'm sorry to hear about the rudeness you experienced while shopping at our store. I wish there was something we could do to prevent such unpleasant events from occurring but, unfortunately, we cannot always observe peculiar behavior in people who come through our store, or intercept them as an incident develops.

I hope this incident will not give you a bad impression of Fashion Fair stores. We value you as a customer, and I look forward to seeing you again.

Sincerely,

Kathy Goodman
Manager

- Express understanding for the customer's feelings.

- Establish that there was nothing you could have done to prevent the rudeness from occurring.

- Express hope that the incident will not affect your customer's patronage and that he or she will try you again.

Company Name
Address
City, State Zip

Date

Mr. Francis D'Attalo
905 Wingate Road
Rochester, NY 14692

Dear Mr. D'Attalo:

Thank you for calling to check on the status of the shirts you ordered from us (Item 53J, Order #29746) three weeks ago (July 28). I have looked into your order, and everything is on schedule. Perhaps you did not notice that on the bottom of the order form we have noted that any items that are monogrammed, such as your shirts, will require a delivery time of four to five weeks instead of the usual two to three weeks.

Your shirts should be arriving next week. I believe that you will be very satisfied with your Wellington Bay shirts. Please let me know if I can be of any further assistance.

Sincerely,

Glenn Hanks
Customer Service

- Clarify what the delivery time is for the order.

- Refer to the item as specifically as possible (Sales# or PO#, etc.).

- Express goodwill and willingness to help out further.

Company Name
Address
City, State Zip

Date

Mr. Jonas Rew
30 Golden Hill Drive
Philadelphia, PA 19140

Dear Mr. Rew:

I've tried to reach you by phone because I feel problems should be dealt with in person. However, I have been unable to catch you at home this last week, and I don't want our disagreement to go on much longer.

I understand from J. C. Gilbert, our stylist, that you were very unhappy with Radar's grooming last Monday. She said you felt we had "dandified" and "emasculated" Radar by putting him in a "business suit." As we discussed when you brought Radar in, Airedales cost $20 more to groom because their clip is very difficult. For example, they must retain "eyebrows," always difficult to achieve with such energetic dogs. During our conversation, I felt you were familiar with the way Airedales looked after they had been clipped. I'm very sorry for the misunderstanding.

Nevertheless, I must insist you pay your account in full. We spent considerable time removing burrs and snarls and gave Radar a flea bath as well as clipping him. I'm afraid the aesthetics of the cut have no bearing on the necessity to pay for work performed.

I look forward to receiving your check for $40.00 as soon as possible.

Sincerely,

Lyman Gordon

- Acknowledge that the customer may have misunderstood, and detail clearly the work performed, but firmly insist on your right to payment.

Company Name
Address
City, State Zip

Date

Miss Karen Steinkraus
289 Holden Avenue
Lansdowne, PA 19050

Dear Miss Steinkraus:

Along with this letter, I'm sending back the sheets (Sales #4503) that you returned to us. I'm sorry to hear that they were not the color you expected, especially since there were color swatches as well as color photographs of the sheets in the catalog. Unfortunately, as we have indicated in large type on the bottom of our order form, we cannot accept any items for return or exchange that have been monogrammed, unless there is a defect in either the material or workmanship.

I apologize for the inconvenience our policy has caused you. Thank you for your understanding.

Sincerely,

Paul Hatfield
Sales Manager

Enclosure

- Outline the terms of sale specifically and indicate where that information is located in the sales literature that the customer already has (e.g., the order form, the catalog).

- Clarify the misunderstanding.

- Express goodwill.

Company Name
Address
City, State Zip

Date

Mr. George Stang
2500 Chardon Rd.
Willoughby, OH 44094

Dear Mr. Stang:

I am sorry to hear you are dissatisfied with the capacity of your Patsy Ice Cream Maker, Model IC-BIG, which makes one quart. I cannot understand why you thought it would make a half-gallon since our ad, the box and the owner's manual clearly state the quantity that each operating cycle will produce is one quart.

I think that your using the Patsy Model IC-BIG you will find that the one quart capacity is quite convenient. Also, since the operating cycle is only 30 minutes, another batch can be prepared quickly.

Sincerely,

Carmen Linn
Customer Service

- Clarify the misunderstanding by stating the product specifications and where the information can be found in the sales literature.

- If possible, explain why the product specifications are positive features.

Company Name
Address
City, State Zip

Date

Mrs. Aileen Yamamoto
372 Center Street
Granada Hills, CA 91344

Dear Mrs. Yamamoto:

I have received your letter concerning the A-Pro 1900 hairdryer that you recently purchased. I'm sorry that you misunderstood the product specifications. As indicated in the sales literature, the hairdryer is designed to be used only on 115 volts, 60 hertz electrical current; it cannot be used on 220 volts, 50 hertz current.

Our policy is to accept authorized returns within 30 days of purchase if the product is returned in the original box. I have enclosed a shipping label for your convenience.

If you wish, we will send you a refund check for $28.95 upon receipt of the hairdryer. However, if you are interested in a hairdryer that runs on 220 volts, 50 hertz electrical current, I suggest the A-Pro 2400 model. It is very similar to the A-Pro 1900 and lists for the same price, $28.95. We also carry a model that can be used on both 115 volts and 220 volts, the A-Pro 3500. It is extremely popular and lists for $36.95. Please write me or call our toll-free, 24-hour number, (800) 991-6000, if you wish to make arrangements about either of these models. We can ship the 2400 model at no cost to you or the 3500 model upon receipt of an additional $8.00 (in both cases, upon receipt of the 1900 model you now have).

Sincerely,

Tim Comcheck
Customer Service

Enclosure

- Acknowledge the customer's specific complaint and state the courses of action available.

- If you have other products that fit the customer's needs, steer the customer toward them. The customer will be more satisfied, and you'll have kept the sale.

Company Name
Address
City, State Zip

Date

Miss Krista Hemeyer
206 Peachtree Lane
Athens, GA 30613

Dear Miss Hemeyer:

I'm sorry to hear of the damage to your A-Pro 1900 hairdryer during your trip to Italy. Unfortunately, we cannot be held responsible for this damage, which occurred because the hairdryer was plugged into a 220 volt, 50 hertz electrical outlet. As specifically indicated on the box, on the documentation inside the box, and on the actual product, the A-Pro 1900 is designed to be used only on 115 volt, 60 hertz electrical current. No return is therefore possible.

Sincerely yours,

Tom Comcheck
Customer Service

- Clarify the product specifications and indicate where they can be found in the sales literature.

- Explain why no return is possible.

Company Name
Address
City, State Zip

Date

Mr. Robert Metz
Euclid Orthopedic Group
358 Euclid Avenue
Euclid, OH 44117

Dear Mr. Metz:

I'm glad to hear that you are pleased with the quality of sharpening that EdgeTech has provided. I hope that you will give us the opportunity to serve you again.

I'd like to clarify a misunderstanding we may have had regarding delivery terms and turn-around time. The rates that we quoted you for the sharpening of your surgical instruments is based on the normal Wednesday afternoon pickup from your office and delivery to your office on the following Monday morning by our representative. If you require a pickup other than on Wednesday afternoon, there is a special charge of $10.00 per order, but the sharpening price is still the same as quoted per surgical instrument. If you require an overnight turnaround, there is again a special pickup charge of $10.00 and, in addition, the sharpening rates are 15% above the regular quoted rates.

Please let me know if you have any questions. I look forward to your business.

Sincerely,

Jason Green
Account Manager

- Specifically state the delivery terms in question and clarify the misunderstanding.

- Express appreciation for the business.

Company Name
Address
City, State Zip

Date

Ms. Eileen Johnson
42 Ferry Lane
Concord, NH 03301

Dear Ms. Johnson:

Larry Crosby, our Credit and Collections Manager, has told me of your intense dissatisfaction with the way your father's recent auto repair was handled here in our shop.

I am terribly sorry that you and your family have had these difficulties. Please be sure that I will give the entire matter a very thorough review. Mr. Johnson's repairs were extremely complicated. It will take me some time to review this with the mechanics involved and the Shop Manager, but after I have completed my investigation, I would very much like to meet with you and your father to discuss the problem he experienced. Is there a possibility that you will be visiting your parents over the holidays? If so, perhaps we can arrange a mutually convenient time to meet.

I asked Mr. Crosby to hold up any further collection proceedings until I have discussed the matter with you and your father in person. I will be in touch as soon as I have completed my review. I would appreciate your speaking to your attorney as soon as possible to delay the legal action he contemplates—that would serve no one's best interests.

Sincerely yours,

Pierce Franklin Thomas
General Manager

- No one really wants legal action. Try to forestall it by offering to establish the facts and have a face-to-face discussion.

- The tone should be reasonable but not apologetic. You do not know if your company is at fault or what action you wish to take if it is. Do not make specific reference to the "facts." If they disagree with the customer's version, you'll engender hostility.

Credit and Collections 5

Strangely enough, when matters of credit and collection come up, businesspeople often forget that they are writing to other human beings. More than that, they forget that they are writing to *customers*, people whose business they value. It is absolutely essential that you treat everyone with courtesy and understanding, and that includes customers who have not paid their bills or customers to whom you cannot yet extend credit for one reason or another.

In fact, the collection process begins with the sale. Overselling—selling to someone who truly cannot afford an item or a service or to someone who doesn't need the item or service—often creates massive problems later on. Credit and collections are actually part of the selling process, since the sale is not really complete until the seller receives payment.

Credit letters. Many people have been offended or hurt by the way creditors have dealt with them in the past. As a result, refusing credit is a very ticklish issue, and the tone of any letter should be extremely sensitive. Offering to provide credit after the customer has established a track record is a good way to present the bad news positively. Remember, though, that you do no one a favor if you extend credit to someone who is truly not creditworthy.

Collection letters. To avoid having to write collection letters in the first place, make it as easy as possible for the customer to pay on time by offering discounts for timely payment, by providing self-addressed envelopes, or by making it an option to charge the payment to a major credit card. The easier you make it, the more likely you are to get what you want—first, attention to your bill among the plethora of pieces anyone receives in the course of the day and second, actual and prompt payment.

If your customer is late in paying, however, you need to establish an automatic sequence of collection letters. It has been documented that the longer the customer goes without paying, the less likely you are to see any payment, even if you turn the account over to a collection agency. Collection sequences follow a standard pattern—notification or reminder, inquiry, appeal, demand, ultimatum. It's correct to start any collection sequence with a notification that payment has not been received (a statement of fact) and an inquiry as to whether a problem exists.

Despite all the "the check is in the mail" jokes, someone may not have paid because of events beyond his or her control. The U. S. Postal Service may be at fault or the business or person may have moved or be on vacation. If a personal tragedy has occurred (a death in the family perhaps), sending a hostile letter will not only lose you a customer, but may blacken your reputation with other potential customers.

Of course, if you ask people whether there's a problem, they may actually respond by calling and telling you what it is. Although this is precisely what you want (you want to keep the communication going at almost any cost), you'll need to have someone available to talk with them and possibly to negotiate an extended payment schedule.

If your reminder and/or inquiry doesn't work (the two letters are frequently combined), then you'll need to have a letter that appeals to the customer's sense of fair play. You have provided a service or a product; the customer owes you something in return. You then proceed to demanding payment and to an ultimate threat to turn the account over to a collection agency. At each stage, though, whether you adopt the moderate tone of the first sequence of letters or the stern tone of the second sequence, keep your determination to treat the customer with sensitivity and honesty. Treating a slow payer with politeness is difficult, but the ability to do so may preserve that customer's goodwill in the future.

Company Name
Address
City, State Zip

Date

Mr. George Maxham
265 Coast Boulevard
Jenner, CA 95450

Dear Mr. Maxham:

We're pleased to hear you'd like to establish a credit account with
H. R. Stoneham Corporation and look forward to the opportunity to
serve you on an ongoing basis.

We do require that credit applicants complete the enclosed application
form before receiving formal credit approval. Once we've received your
completed form we'll notify you within three weeks regarding its
acceptance.

If you have any questions about the form or our approval requirements,
please call me at 1-800-268-4269. I will be pleased to help you provide
the information we need.

Yours truly,

Marion Stanley
Credit Manager

Enclosure

- Use a cordial tone to maintain a good relationship with an existing or potential customer and let the customer know you appreciate the patronage.

- Specify when the applicant can expect a decision.

- Let the applicant know how to request assistance.

Company Name
Address
City, State Zip

Date

Mr. Richard Miller
MZM Incorporated
116 Brookpark Road
Houston, TX 77055

Dear Mr. Miller:

Thank you for your purchase order ST-1950. So that we may extend our normal terms of net 30 days, please furnish us with the following information:

1. your annual report
2. name of your bank, account number, and contact
3. names of two suppliers with whom you are presently doing business.

We look forward to serving you, and we feel that extending 30-day payment terms is part of that service. Thank you for your cooperation, and for your order.

Sincerely,

Bill Small
Credit Manager

- Ask for the information (be specific) you need to make a good decision. Remember, it's your money that they are asking to use!

- Express appreciation for their cooperation and for their business.

Company Name
Address
City, State Zip

Date

Ms. Martha Johanneson
Manager, Credit Department
Northrop Department Stores
Nashua, NH 03060

Dear Ms. Johanneson:

Thomas Slate (Acct. #2276052) has named your company as a credit reference in his application for an account with our store. We are now reviewing Mr. Slate's application and would appreciate your providing the following information regarding your experience as one of Mr. Slate's creditors:

- length of credit relationship
- amounts billed monthly and annually
- promptness in payment/delinquency

As soon as we receive this information, we can complete processing Mr. Slate's account. We would appreciate your prompt reply.

Thank you.

Sincerely,

Harold Lowe
Credit Department

- Give the name and account number of applicant.

- Specify information you need.

- Ask for prompt action, noting the importance of the report in your decision.

Company Name
Address
City, State Zip

Date

Mr. Calvin McCormick
Credit Manager
Webster Products, Inc.
4442 Withey Highway
Flint, MI 48503

Dear Mr. McCormick:

One of our credit applicants, Perkins/Neville Associates of Grand Rapids, MI, has named your company as a credit reference. Before extending credit to an applicant, we require information on that applicant's experience with other creditors. Would you please furnish a credit report on Perkins/Neville, including length of relationship, amounts billed annually, and promptness of payment?

We would appreciate your response soon so that we can complete our review of Perkins/Neville's application within a month.

Thank you for your cooperation.

Sincerely,

Stanley Johnson
Credit Department

- Identify the credit applicant about whom you seek information.

- Specify information you need.

- Note the time span in which you need a response.

Company Name
Address
City, State Zip

Date

Ms. Nancy Vosburgh
13 Fairfax Court
Richmond, VA 23225

Dear Ms. Vosburgh:

We at Temple Department Stores are pleased to welcome you as a
Temple Card holder. We think you'll find the Temple Card opens the
door to enjoying many valuable services, including easy credit terms
and advance notice of special sales.

Please validate the enclosed Temple Card by signing your name in ink
in the space indicated on the back. You can then use it when you shop
in any one of our four stores in the greater Richmond area. We have
also enclosed a copy of our credit terms specifying how your account
will be billed each month.

Again, welcome to our family of Temple Card Holders!

Sincerely,

Merrill Cottle
Billing Department

Enclosure

- Cordially welcome the new credit customer.

- State what the customer needs to know/do before using the account.

- Include written notice of credit terms.

Company Name
Address
City, State Zip

Date

Mr. Jack Martin
Yankee Modular Homes
72 Quincy Road
Boston, MA 02127

Dear Mr. Martin:

Thank you for your recent order. We have a long history of serving new businesses. Your initiative in providing low-cost homes in an urban setting is bound to draw a large clientele.

Because a steady cash flow is important to us, however, we approve very few credit accounts. Although the credit reference you provided is favorable, you will need to establish two more credit references to charge orders exceeding $1,000.

We do, though, offer a 5% discount on cash orders. Please indicate on the enclosed copy of your order form whether you want to place a cash order now.

We will review your application in three months. If at that time you have established additional references, we will accept a credit order.

We wish you the best of luck in your new endeavor.

Sincerely,

John Snyder
Vice President, Accounting

- Credit is refused for a variety of reasons. A regular customer may have fallen behind in payment. A young credit candidate or new business may have no credit history. A customer may have a history of being delinquent on credit payments.

- Exercise good judgment in refusing a candidate for credit to avoid legal action.

Refusal of Credit, Retail (5-07)

Company Name
Address
City, State Zip

Date

Ms. Katherine Woodley
14 Elmhurst Street
Marietta, GA 30086

Dear Ms. Woodley:

Thank you for showing your interest in becoming a Thomas Furniture Mart credit account holder. We're happy to know you appreciate the fine quality of our merchandise as well as our wide selection of contemporary and traditional home furnishings.

We've received your application and are sorry that we cannot extend you credit at this time. One of our requirements for credit is that applicants have lived in the area for at least one year. As a newcomer to Marietta, you do not meet that requirement.

We hope, though, that you will continue to shop at Thomas's and that you will resubmit your application after you have met our residency requirement.

Sincerely,

Perron F. Towers
Credit Manager

- Thank the customer for the application.

- Refuse the request graciously and regretfully.

- Specify *why* the application was refused.

- Invite the applicant to try again should circumstances change.

Company Name
Address
City, State Zip

Date

Mr. W. G. Randall
Purchasing Agent
P&W Leasing Company
200 Fairwood Lane
Detroit, MI 48215

Dear Mr. Randall:

As of March 31, we have not received your February payment. Have you forgotten? Please check your records.

If you have already sent your payment, please disregard this notice and accept our thanks for your payment.

Sincerely,

W. P. Johnson
Collection Manager

- A first reminder for payment reflects your understanding that some minor problem may have delayed payment. You assume that the customer has every intention of paying and needs only to be reminded.

Company Name
Address
City, State Zip

Date

Mr. W. G. Randall
Purchasing Agent
P&W Leasing Company
200 Fairwood Lane
Detroit, MI 48215

Dear Mr. Randall:

You have been a valued customer for many years, and you have always been conscientious about paying your bills within the 30-day payment period.

Your good credit rating has enabled you to purchase from us on convenient payment terms at a substantial discount. Because of your prompt payment record, we have been glad to serve as a reference when you have applied for credit with other suppliers.

To keep your good credit rating and to continue receiving a substantial discount, payment of your account is necessary. Are you having some problem that we can help you with?

By sending your check for $350.00 in the enclosed stamped envelope, you will bring your account up-to-date and protect your credit rating. If this is not feasible, please call or write me today.

Sincerely,

W. P. Johnson
Collection Manager

Enclosure

- As frustrating as it is to send out a reminder and still get no response, assume that the customer has overlooked your payment request, or that other circumstances are preventing payment.

- Be specific as to the payment required and make it easy for the customer to pay you (the return envelope).

Company Name
Address
City, State Zip

Date

Mr. W. G. Randall
Purchasing Agent
P&W Leasing Company
200 Fairwood Lane
Detroit, MI 48215

Dear Mr. Randall:

This morning I received your file with a big OVERDUE stamped on it. I receive customer files only when some serious problem has occurred.

Your order was shipped over four months ago, and we still have not received a payment from you. As you are in business, Mr. Randall, you must realize that we cannot afford to carry this debt on our books any longer.

To preserve your credit privileges, please do one of the following:

- Remit the full amount of $350.00 today.
- Send us $150.00 as partial payment, with the balance payable by June 30.
- Explain your situation, and let us know what you can do to meet your obligation.

Your immediate response is necessary.

Sincerely,

Mark Bowman
President

- Avoid overt threats, but convey your desire to collect the overdue payment immediately. Having a senior company official sign the letter will signal urgency.

- Allow the customer to make a payment without losing face.

Company Name
Address
City, State Zip

Date

Mr. W. G. Randall
Purchasing Agent
P&W Leasing Company
200 Fairwood Lane
Detroit, MI 48215

Dear Mr. Randall:

We are sending this letter to you with regret that previous efforts to obtain payment of your account have been unsuccessful.

We sent a bill for $350.00 for payment by March 1. Over the past four months, we have tried to get you to fulfill your obligations to us. We assumed, since you had an excellent credit rating and have always been responsible in paying your bills before, that some small oversight was to blame.

Please send us your payment for the overdue bill within five days so that we do not have to turn your account over to a collection agency.

Sincerely,

Mark Bowman
President

- Do not send an ultimatum unless you are able to back it up. By sending this letter, you can encourage customers to reevaluate their priorities. If their finances are in disorder, you will not get results until this stage.

- You are no longer interested in excuses, but only want your payment.

Company Name
Address
City, State Zip

Date

Mr. and Mrs. Lawrence Sternin
1246 South Branch Parkway
Westwood, NJ 07675

Dear Mr. and Mrs. Sternin:

We're delighted you're enjoying your new living room furniture, including our popular Relax-a-lounger. However, it has been two months now since we delivered your furniture, and we have yet to receive your payment for $2,375.60 (Invoice #46237, copy enclosed). Have you already put a check in the mail to us?

If not, please give this matter your attention today, since we want to be able to extend you credit the next time you shop for quality home furnishings.

Sincerely,

Claire McManus
Billing Department
555-3222, ext. 102

Enclosure

• A polite, cordial reminder encourages the customer to settle the matter immediately. You want to be paid *and* keep the customer.

Company Name
Address
City, State Zip

Date

Mr. and Mrs. Lawrence Sternin
1246 South Branch Parkway
Westwood, NJ 07675

Dear Mrs. and Mrs. Sternin:

Unfortunately, we still haven't received your $2,375.60 payment
for merchandise you purchased January 5 (Invoice #46237, dated
January 12). Because your account is three months past due, we are
now forced to add a late charge of $23.75 in accordance with our credit
policy. The new balance is $2,399.35.

Please be sure to settle your account with us today. If you have
difficulty paying the full amount now, please call me today to discuss
arranging a payment schedule.

Yours truly,

Claire McManus
Billing Department
555-3222, ext. 102

- Note *how* and *why* late charges were assessed.

- Offer to adjust the payment schedule. It's better to get the money slowly than not at all.

Company Name
Address
City, State Zip

Date

Mr. and Mrs. Lawrence Sternin
1246 South Branch Parkway
Westwood, NJ 07675

Dear Mr. and Mrs. Sternin:

Your letter has been referred to me by Claire McManus of our Billing
Department. Because you have failed to make any payment on Invoice
#46237 for $2,399.35 (including late charges) or to contact us to
arrange a payment schedule, we have been forced to initiate
procedures to repossess the furniture you bought at our store.

We will be contacting you to arrange a date for repossession if we do
not receive full payment from you within two weeks. Please make every
effort to ensure that we are not forced to take this drastic action.

Sincerely,

R. Lane Peterson
Executive Vice President

- Have the collection letter written by someone high in the company and threaten action only after repeated attempts to secure payment have failed and the customer has shown no intention of cooperating.

- Note that you regret the severity of your action, which leaves the door open for the customer to settle.

Company Name
Address
City, State Zip

Date

Mr. and Mrs. Lawrence Sternin
1246 South Branch Parkway
Westwood, NJ 07675

Dear Mr. and Mrs. Sternin:

Regrettably, we are forced to repossess the five items of furniture we delivered to you on January 5, due to your failure to pay the $2,399.35 you owe for them.

On May 5, representatives of our company will arrive at your home at 10 a.m. to collect:

(1) queen-size sleep sofa (model 206G)
(1) "Corona" coffee table
(2) "Corona" end tables
(1) "Relax-a-lounger" (model 460L)

We had hoped to avoid this extreme action by offering you flexible credit options to lessen the difficulty you face making payments. However, your unwillingness to cooperate with our billing department has left us no choice.

Sincerely,

R. Lane Peterson
Executive Vice President

- When notifying a customer of intent to repossess, list the items involved and set a date for repossession.

- Send the letter via certified mail, return receipt, so you will have evidence that the customer was aware of your intentions.

Company Name
Address
City, State Zip

Date

Mr. and Mrs. Lawrence Sternin
1246 South Branch Parkway
Westwood, NJ 07675

Dear Mr. and Mrs. Sternin:

We were unhappy to find that we could not gain admittance (to take delivery of our merchandise) when our representatives arrived at your home on May 5. R. Lane Peterson, our chief financial officer, has turned over your file to me, and, as president of the company, I have decided that legal action is necessary.

Our decision to repossess our merchandise came only after several months of our repeated attempts to come to payment terms with you. Your continuing lack of cooperation leaves us no choice but to turn this matter over to the County Sheriff's office for resolution. All our future efforts to contact you will be through that office.

Sincerely,

William Travis
President

- As a last resort, refer the matter to law enforcement authorities.

- Having the company president write the final letter underlines the gravity of the situation and demonstrates that everyone in authority has considered the matter carefully.

Company Name
Address
City, State Zip

Date

Mr. Edward Bonnard
Equitable Credit Check
6789 Loyola Drive
San Jose, CA 95125

Dear Mr. Bonnard:

Kindly include this letter in our company's credit file. Although in the main the material you summarized is correct, your summary does not provide a clear picture of the history of our business and therefore may be misinterpreted by lenders.

Our company, Simple Tools, has actually been in business since December 31, 1976. However, for the first five years, it was known as Thomas Canner, DBA Simple Tools. We incorporated as Simple Tools, Inc., on December 31, 1981, and that is the date you give for the inception of the business.

I look forward to receiving a revised summary including this additional information.

Sincerely,

Thomas Canner
President

- Credit bureaus must include pertinent information in their files if that information is verifiably correct. It's worthwhile to check occasionally to make sure that their files are complete and accurate.

- Always request written verification that a change has been made.

Company Name
Address
City, State Zip

Date

Ms. Leila Foxx
Equitable Credit Check
6789 Loyola Drive
San Jose, CA 95125

Dear Ms. Foxx:

As I stated on the phone, the information in your files relating to our mortgage payment history is erroneous. As you can see from the attached statements provided by Howland Savings Bank, the holder of our mortgage, we have never been notified of foreclosure proceedings, as stipulated in your file. In fact, our company's payment record is exemplary, as you can clearly see.

I will look forward to seeing a new synopsis of our company, indicating that this grossly false statement has been corrected, and to seeing, as you promised on the phone, copies of letters detailing the correct information to all those who have made inquiries about our credit standing.

Sincerely,

Georgia T. Kroner
Vice President, Finance

Attachments

- A good credit rating is vital in business. If you learn of a false statement, ensure that the credit bureau corrects it as soon as possible and that they send correction statements to anyone they have misinformed.

Dealing with Suppliers 6

The most important thing you can remember when writing letters to suppliers is to be clear. Tell your reader exactly what you need and when you expect it, or what you are going to provide and when. When making requests for information, as in inquiring about credit terms, you will help yourself by making the request as specific as possible. If you take the time to think through your needs and communicate them clearly to the supplier, you have a better chance of receiving a precise answer and, therefore, a better opportunity of making a sound business decision. Compliments and suggestions should be direct and unambiguous; don't get bogged down in flowery platitudes or general observations.

Are we speaking the same language? These days, people in business are constantly confronted with terminology and jargon. Refer to merchandise in the supplier's terms, use dates and numbers from invoices and bills of lading in your correspondence and, if necessary, look up the name of the part in the manual so that it is correctly identified in your communications. Be sure everyone knows what is going on.

Referring to invoice numbers, recalling dates and stating exact amounts is particularly important when your letter is expressing dissatisfaction. Command of these routine items demonstrates that you have looked into the matter carefully, have weighed the possibilities, and still find something unsatisfactory. A supplier who wants to keep your business will be more likely to see your side of a problem if you are precise, while remaining reasonable in tone.

I'm sorry, you're sorry. When you are inconvenienced by a supplier, remember that *your* company may inconvenience someone somewhere along the line. The best thing you can do is to assume that everyone wants to do a good job. Respect the professionalism of every supplier and insist that they respect your professionalism, too. This will create the best working environment for everyone.

Company Name
Address
City, State Zip

Date

Ms. Samantha Willis
Sales Representative
Fabrics First Incorporated
12 Calico Plaza
Darien, CT 06820

Dear Samantha:

Both the "Garden Chintz" pillow line and your new specialty quilts are selling almost faster than we can keep them in stock. Since your products seem so popular with our customers, we are interested in carrying other items of a style and quality similar to that of the pillows and quilts—perhaps table accessories or throw rugs. Please send brochures and price information on any of these types of products you now have, and I will then call you to discuss an order.

Sincerely,

Ramona Thomas
Purchasing Manager

- If you're particularly happy with a certain product, let the supplier know.

- Be as specific as you can about the kinds of products about which you want more information.

Company Name
Address
City, State Zip

Date

Mr. Ed Kelton
Kelton's House and Window Cleaning Service
345 Percheron Drive
Melbourne, FL 32935

Dear Mr. Kelton:

As we discussed on the phone, we look forward to your providing office-cleaning services every Tuesday and Friday evening (beginning May 17). To ensure you're paid regularly and promptly, we'd like to be billed on the last day of each month for the services you have provided that month. We will then pay each bill within 30 days of the date we receive it.

We hope this credit arrangement is satisfactory to you. If not, please call me to discuss alternatives.

Yours truly,

Roger Palmer
964-3321

- State the circumstances of your agreement with the supplier.

- Specify the credit terms you would like to establish.

- Leave the door open for discussion if your suggestion does not satisfy the supplier.

Inquiry about Credit Terms (6-03)

Company Name
Address
City, State Zip

Date

Mr. Gordon Harvey
Harvey Power Equipment
1220 Brookhaven Blvd.
Augusta, GA 30906

Dear Mr. Harvey:

Good Earth and Lawn is expanding its services this year to include the northern half of the city. We have serviced residential and commercial accounts in the southern neighborhoods for the past nine years. I have enclosed a list of our larger accounts.

For our expansion, and to upgrade existing equipment, we will need three (3) 12 h.p. riding mowers (36" rotary), four (4) self-propelled mowers (20" rotary) and two (2) weed and brush cutters.

As I'm sure you can understand, there will be a time lag between our initial use of the equipment and our receipt of fees for work performed. I would, therefore, appreciate receiving information regarding your firm's billing and credit terms.

Thank you.

Sincerely,

Miles Templeton

- Mention (for the supplier's benefit) your company's background; put yourself in as good a light as possible.

- Specify what type of goods or services you're considering buying. Explain why you want credit.

Company Name
Address
City, State Zip

Date

Ms. Yvonne Frost
Peerless Dry Cleaners
2507 Durango Dr.
Billings, MT 59101

Dear Ms. Frost:

Several of our waiters at the Lucky Seven Restaurant, on Main Street in Billings, have told us of the superior drycleaning service you offer. We have now agreed to provide weekly uniform drycleaning to all of our staff members and are interested in contracting for these services. We would like to deliver approximately 25 uniforms (shirts and trousers) for cleaning each Tuesday morning and have them returned to us by noon the following day.

Before we decide on a particular service, we need to know what discount you are prepared to offer for this type of order and what the weekly charge per uniform would be. Would you please call me by Wednesday with this information?

Sincerely,

Bart Tolland
443-7627

- Suppliers like to know where their business comes from—do mention any referrals from satisfied customers.

- Estimate as closely as possible the volume and regularity of the service or goods you require. This information is essential in figuring discounts.

Company Name
Address
City, State Zip

Date

Sales Manager
Croft Office Systems
75 Main Street
West Orange, NJ 07052

Dear Sales Manager:

Our secretarial service company will be upgrading our word processors.
We would like you to quote the following for immediate delivery:

Quantity	Description
(2)	Macintosh SE computers
(2)	2400 Baud modems
(1)	Laserwriter
(1)	300 dpi scanner

Your bid, including payment terms and/or credit options, should be
submitted to me no later than Friday, July 28.

Sincerely,

David Pierce
Manager

- Be specific about what you want them to bid on (including quantities and the projected delivery date), when they are to respond, and to whom they are to send the bid.

- Ask about payment terms, as these may influence your purchasing decision.

Company Name
Address
City, State Zip

Date

Mr. David Lewis
XYCOMA Telecommunications
59-304 Hapaki Street
Aiea, HI 96701

Dear Mr. Lewis:

We're sorry to inform you that we did not choose your products for the PBX expansion for our Honolulu office. Your preferred delivery cycle of 18 weeks is too long, given our specified requirement of 12 weeks. Your quote for the 12-week delivery cycle was about 10% higher than the successful bidder.

Thank you, however, for the detailed bid you provided. We will be sure to call you when we have telecommunications needs in the future.

Sincerely,

Kathy Gandalf
Office Manager

- Writing this type of letter is not pleasant, but should not be put off.

- Tell a company why it was not selected, if it is constructive.

- Be cordial and thank them for their effort (you want them to quote again).

Company Name
Address
City, State Zip

Date

Mr. Fred Costello
Costello Castings Corp.
57 North Drive
Akron, OH 44301

Dear Mr. Costello:

Thank you for your letter and for your interest in supplying castings for our brake assemblies. Since yours is a new company and because our tolerances are so exact, we would have to see more of a track record before we consider you as a supplier. In addition, our turn-around times are quite demanding, so we would need more references than you can provide at this time.

We are, however, always looking for reliable new suppliers, and I would be interested in hearing from you again in about six months, when you've gotten through the start-up phase.

Sincerely,

Jeff Craven
Manager

- Be specific about why you are refusing to do business.

- If there's a possibility that you might do business with them in the future, let them know when to contact you again.

Company Name
Address
City, State Zip

Date

Mr. William Carabetta
Bath Bazaar
3678 Cumberland Pike
Nashville, TN 37228

Dear Mr. Carabetta:

On March 25, you installed a Jet Splash 20 hot tub in our hotel. For two weeks, the tub functioned perfectly, giving our guests many hours of relaxing bathing. In the past week, however, we've had problems with the tub's water-heating mechanism. We have been unable to raise the tub's water temperature higher than 75 degrees Fahrenheit.

We would like our guests to be able to enjoy the tub as they did when it was functioning properly. I believe service and repair calls come under the terms of the tub's warranty and would like to have a service technician come to the hotel as soon as can be arranged. I will call on Friday to determine the first available date.

Thank you.

Yours very truly,

Gordon Cameron
Assistant Manager

- Give all the important details—what you bought, when you bought it.

- Be as specific as possible about the type of problem you're having. Even if you don't know what caused it, describe the symptoms.

- Be clear about how you would like the matter resolved.

Company Name
Address
City, State Zip

Date

Mr. Robert Evans
Concord Office Supplies, Inc.
Bicentennial Drive
Nashua, NH 03060

Dear Mr. Evans:

I am returning with this letter a recent shipment of 2,000 personalized ballpoint pens (order #21392943). Upon examination of the pens, we discovered that our company name had been misspelled. As your records will confirm, the order specified that each pen should read:

Lombardo Limousines
Coach of Kings

Please make the necessary correction and send another shipment of 2,000 pens as soon as possible.

Yours truly,

Carl Lombardo

- Be sure to refer to your order by number.

- State exactly why you were dissatisfied with the quality of the product.

- State how you would like the matter remedied.

Company Name
Address
City, State Zip

Date

Mr. Joseph I. Zale
Zale's Contracting
6624 West High Street
Richmond, VA 23230

Dear Mr. Zale:

We've received your invoice (#2562) for carpentry work in our office. We'd very much like to pay you, but as we discussed on the phone on May 14, there are still several items that must be attended to before the job is finished. These include the countertop formica and the additional shelves in the supply closet. We cannot efficiently run the production side of our business until these tasks are done.

We will be delighted to send you a check when the work is completed.

Sincerely,

Thomas Lotus
Senior Vice President

- The name of this game is "leverage," and you have every right to withhold payment. Putting it in writing will forestall or delay legal action.

Company Name
Address
City, State Zip

Date

Mr. Peter Hyman
Accounts Receivable
South California Medical
4035 Ripley Boulevard
Venice, CA 90291

Dear Mr. Hyman:

We are unable to process your invoice #8092 for disposable linens.
This invoice represents only a portion of our purchase order #42658,
and we cannot pay until the entire purchase order has been filled.

You are correct in thinking that we had a different policy in the past.
Unfortunately, we have had problems with vendors who submitted
invoices for part of a purchase order and later submitted invoices for the
entire purchase order. The resulting confusion forced us to institute a
new policy. Please submit a new invoice as soon as the entire order
has been filled.

Sincerely,

James P. Darrow
Accounts Payable

- Always state the main point first.

- Although clearly you've changed the policy (because of dishonest vendors or ineptness on
  the part of your people), assigning blame is counterproductive. Referring to "confusion" is
  more politic.

Company Name
Address
City, State Zip

Date

Mr. Leonard Mercer
Revere Office Equipment
42 Mercer Road
Natick, MA 01760

Dear Len:

As you can see from the enclosed envelope and your invoice (#3429) for $1,395, your invoice of April 19 was delayed in reaching us because it was addressed to the wrong town. We did not receive it until today.

When I talked with you on the phone about a FAX, you said that the list price for the FAX 103 was $1,795, that Revere's usual price was $1,395, and that you would be able to sell one to us at $1,295. When I visited the store, no one was able to give me an exact price, but I was told that you'd call me when you returned. Since I did not hear from you, I assumed that the $1,295 price would be charged.

I would appreciate it if you would check your records and let me know whether there would be any problem in reissuing the invoice at $1,295. Please note that the invoice should be made out to Totoket Associates and that the mailing address is Box 298, Reading, MA 01867.

Sincerely,

Jamieson Perkins

Enclosure

- In something of this magnitude, "putting it in writing" is essential. Following up with a phone call is also a good idea.

- Decide before sending the letter how rigid or flexible your position is so you'll be prepared to react to the supplier's response.

Company Name
Address
City, State Zip

Date

Miss Rosemary Randolf
Acme Toys for Tots Co.
22 Rider Street
Evanston, IL 60202

Dear Miss Randolf:

Please cancel our order (#1707-56) for 200 "Wooden Animal Puzzles for 2-4 Year Olds." We have just found a large number of these puzzles in our storeroom and do not have need for more at this time. We will place a new order when our present supply runs out.

Yours truly,

Jonathan Evens
Vice President

- Be certain to include the order number and full name of the product.

- If you believe there will be a question about why you are canceling the order, give the reason, particularly if the supplier is a regular one. Courtesy never hurts.

Company Name
Address
City, State Zip

Date

Mr. Ennis Thompson
Customer Service Dept.
Forest Cable Co.
37 Garibaldi Street
St. Louis, MO 63134

Dear Mr. Thompson:

During the past week, Forest Cable technicians have twice failed to keep appointments to install a surge protection system for our computer equipment. On both Tuesday, May 17, and Friday, May 20, I arranged for our data communications supervisor to be on site from 9:00 am to noon to accommodate the schedule of your service crew. On neither day did the installation technician arrive, nor did he call to explain why the appointment had not been kept. This lack of concern has caused us both serious inconvenience and valuable time.

I would like to believe that Forest Cable values our company as a customer, but quite honestly, the events of last week do not support that view. Can I depend on you to arrange dependable installation at our mutual convenience sometime next week? We have enjoyed the services your company has provided in the past and look forward to reestablishing our relationship on a more pleasant footing. I will call you on Friday to arrange the appointment.

Yours truly,

Beth Dowling
Vice President, Operations

- State specifically why you are dissatisfied. Mention the dates and times when service was unsatisfactory (or non-existent).

- Make it clear how you would like to resolve your issues with the supplier and arrange to discuss the matter further.

Company Name
Address
City, State Zip

Mr. Ted Oldey
Parkway Printers
1406 Topstone Parkway
Gaithersburg, MD 20879

Dear Ted:

Enclosed is a check for $4,508.52, covering the balance due on
Purchase Order 788-10 for the recent printing of our catalog.

While I think we both developed a few gray hairs over the printing
difficulties, I have to praise you and your company for being sensitive to
my needs and responding quickly and professionally.

The catalogs look great and we will be needing a new printing in about
two months.

Again, thanks for your cooperation during this difficult situation.

Kindest regards,

Harold Cousins
President

- When things go awry during a project, and the supplier gives his all, it makes sense to tell him you appreciated the help.

- If additional work will be coming his way shortly, tell him so.

Company Name
Address
City, State Zip

Date

Ms. Marianne Murphy
Murphy Employment Agency
2208 Irvine Street
Lowell, MA 01850

Dear Ms. Murphy:

I believe I have a suggestion that will help you and us. If you could test typists before sending them out on a job, we could both be assured that they can do the work they say they can do.

I know you cannot test every individual on every machine, but you could test, and therefore validate their ability, on the several machines you have in your office. You might also ask for references if typists say they had experience on certain machines at certain places.

I hope this idea will be useful to you.

Yours truly,

Marjorie Williams
Office Manager

- Open the letter with a statement that is sufficiently compelling for the recipient to continue to read. People get free advice all the time; they continue reading only when they perceive some personal value.

- If you are writing to someone you deal with personally, show understanding of that person's problem.

Company Name
Address
City, State Zip

Date

Mr. Harry Sarnoff
Food for Thought Caterers
20 Carson Drive
Omaha, NE 68114

Dear Mr. Sarnoff:

Thank you for the wonderful help your entire staff provided in feeding the participants at our annual meeting on April 20. The room looked lovely, the flowers were beautiful, the service was excellent and, most important, Chef Michael's food was exceptional. You more than kept your promise of being "the best in all ways."

You will hear from us again soon.

Yours truly,

Harry Singh
Director of Communications

• Keep it short and sweet but be sure to include, whenever possible, who should be complimented, what that person or people did, and when it happened.

Company Name
Address
City, State Zip

Date

Mr. Carl Sanderson
Sanderson Electrics
2288 Seventh St.
Cambridge, MA 02138

Dear Mr. Sanderson:

You are indeed fortunate to have as dedicated an engineer as William Southwick. Bill worked with me for hours to ensure that our lighting design will now meet our needs. He was concerned that each area of the shop have lighting appropriate to the work that will be done in that area and that, should we alter the production flow, we will be able to alter the lighting as well.

I have told Bill how much I appreciate his attention to detail, but I wanted to tell you as well. If you feel it is appropriate, feel free to include this letter in his personnel file.

Yours truly,

Harold Wolfson
Construction Coordinator

- Be sure to include the name of the employee and a brief description of what the employee did that you found especially helpful.

- If you are writing to a large organization, you might ask that your letter be added to the individual's personnel file or send a copy to the person you are complimenting.

Company Name
Address
City, State Zip

Date

Mr. Douglas Vreelander
Manum Custom Parts, Inc.
Central Manufacturing Park
Camden, NJ 08122

Dear Mr. Vreelander:

Enclosed is our check #3098 for $3,097.62, which covers the balance
due on invoice #28602. I believe this will bring our account up to date
until we receive the shipment of parts due next month.

Sincerely,

Christopher Worth
Accounting Department

Enclosure

- Be sure to note your check number, the amount of the check, and the invoice your payment covers.

- Confirm that this payment brings your account up-to-date.

Sender's Name
Address
City, State Zip

Date

Mr. Paul Carlson
Carlson and Maxwell Travel Consultants, Ltd.
185 4th Avenue
New Rochelle, NY 10802

Dear Mr. Carlson:

Enclosed is our check #6714 for $789.55, covering the extra charges for the off-site planning meeting that Apex held at the Long Pond Conference Center last month. We apologize for the lateness of this check, but we had to wait for Long Pond to send us the paperwork on our two extra attendees before we could process your invoice (#AP-4948).

I hope that the delay has not caused you any inconvenience.

Sincerely,

Marilyn Stephenson
Accounts Payable

Enclosure

- Be sure to state the number and amount of the check enclosed.

- Apologize for the delay and explain it briefly.

Company Name
Address
City, State Zip

Date

Mrs. Helena Purcell
Creative Custom Catering
26 Muzzey Street
Lexington, MA 02173

Dear Mrs. Purcell:

All who attended the annual fund raising luncheon last Friday remarked on the exquisite buffet. Our thanks to you for providing such a memorable feast.

We received your bill for $4,672.00 (#266084) yesterday. Enclosed is a check for $2,500.00 toward the balance of our account. Because we are entirely dependent on membership contributions for meeting our expenses, we are forced to pay the remaining $2,172.00 next month, when our fund drive has ended.

I regret that we cannot pay the entire amount due today and hope you understand our situation and the reason for the delay.

Sincerely,

Carol Fontana
Vice President

Enclosure

- Express appreciation for good service provided.

- Refer to the invoice by number and propose an alternate payment schedule, giving the reason why you need more time.

- Express regret for not paying more promptly.

Company Name
Address
City, State Zip

Date

Mr. Royce Flaherty
Renshaw Card Company
60 Horse Hill Road
Purchase, NY 10577

Dear Mr. Flaherty:

I have enclosed our final payment of $310.76 (check #6490) for 29,750 of the cards you shipped to us last year. Please apply the payment against the balance on the original invoice #2308.

As we agreed last year, we are paying for the cards on an as-used basis, returning any unused cards for credit. There are 20,250 cards remaining from the 50,000 you shipped us last year. Please let me know how we should arrange to return them to you for credit.

Sincerely,

Terry Getman

Enclosure

- Identify for your reader exactly what figures you are basing your payment on (if it's different from the balance on the invoice).

- Give invoice number and any other relevant information.

- Ask how to proceed with returns (next steps).

Company Name
Address
City, State Zip

Date

Mr. Arnold Smythe
Nature Collectibles
Box 780
Burlington, VT 05405

Dear Mr. Smythe:

When we examined 2 of the 36 sets of Animal Family Figurines that your carrier, Apex Trucking, delivered last Wednesday, May 4, we were dismayed to find several figurines in two sets had arrived broken. I would like to arrange to have the sets with broken figurines returned to you as proof of damage.

Please credit our account for the two sets that were broken. Apart from this problem, we were very pleased with this new addition to your line and hope to reorder in the near future.

Sincerely,

Ivana Robertson
Collectibles Department

- Specify how many items arrived damaged and describe the damage.

- State how you'd like the matter handled.

- Call attention to any possible billing situation.

Company Name
Address
City, State Zip

Date

Ms. Jessica Chasen
Q-Design Art Supplies, Inc.
2600 Mercer Blvd.
Seattle, WA 98124

Dear Ms. Chasen:

Enclosed are 24 pads of Strathmore Parchment Calligraphy Writing
Paper that were mistakenly shipped to us on April 2 (invoice #578657).
Ordering by phone from Lisa Roberts on March 30, we asked for 24
pads of white calligraphy paper. Please accept the parchment paper for
return and send us 24 pads of the white as soon as possible.

Thank you for rectifying this matter promptly.

Sincerely,

Harriet Peters
Office Manager

Enclosures

- Specify what you were sent as well as what should have been sent.

- Include all necessary information: dates, invoice numbers, the name of the person with
  whom you placed the order.

- Be sure to state how you'd like the matter handled.

Company Name
Address
City, State Zip

Date

Ms. Aliza Trocfel
Computer Supply Corp.
415 Main St.
Ridgefield, CT 06877

Dear Ms. Trocfel:

When the Data Defender Diskette File (our PO #698) you shipped to us on March 12 (invoice #2049037) arrived, we were dismayed to find that it had been damaged in transit. The plastic cover was cracked. Please let me know how you would like it returned and send us a replacement as soon as possible.

Thank you for handling this matter promptly.

Sincerely,

Osborne Stallings
Vice President

Enclosures

- Specify what item(s) you were sent and exactly how it was damaged.

- Include all necessary information: dates, purchase order and invoice numbers.

- Be sure to state how you'd like the matter handled.

Personnel Relations 7

Many people have become so fearful of employer-employee relations that they avoid putting anything in writing because they feel it may come back to haunt them. But all the same reasons for putting things in writing discussed in the introduction to this book apply equally to writing in the personnel area. Acrimonious disputes can be avoided if everyone understands hiring practices, job evaluation practices, and other policies and procedures that the company follows. Avoiding these disputes saves immense amounts of time and emotional capital.

The trade-off, of course, is that written practices do constrain employers, even though any policy can be changed at any time with appropriate notice. In practice, changing a "perk" is difficult to do. One entrepreneur cites the story of giving everyone a turkey for the holidays in his first year of business and the nightmare it grew into some years down the road when he found himself with several hundred employees, each waiting for his or her turkey. The moral here is to try to envision your company as it will be in a few years when you think about appropriate policies and procedures.

Hiring and references. From posting a job opening to writing a job confirmation letter, writing is part of the hiring process. Your first step is to think through what the job entails in terms of responsibilities and duties and then to develop a list of the skills necessary to do that job. Many people list very high qualifications (typing speed, college degree) as a way of screening people. One office manager says, "If a person has the discipline to learn to type 75 words per minute, I can teach him or her to do anything else required on the job." A good way to appraise realistically what the job involves is to talk with the person who currently holds the job, or to others in firms similar to yours if the position is new. Doing this preliminary spadework will allow you to write an announcement of a job opening or a job description. If you don't want to get the protest "but that's not in my job description," you may want to add "and other duties as assigned" to cover yourself.

Most managers hate the interviewing process. An interview outline can help immensely because it provides structure to the conversation and helps keep the interviewer in control.

A letter confirming or revising a job offer has contractual implications and should be looked over by an attorney. Be careful not to stipulate anything more than the salary and the starting date. If you have discussed a probationary period, you may also wish to include that in the letter. However, put nothing in the letter that has not been discussed in person. If you do, you're likely to poison the atmosphere of trust you have presumably tried to establish.

References should be handled with finesse. Sound too glowing and you're likely to be disbelieved, too negative and you might seem bitter or personally involved. Keep a reference factual, but if an employee was less than satisfactory, what you don't say can take on as much meaning as what you do say.

Problems. If you have a problem employee, your first step is to talk with the person. Discuss how performance has been falling short of expectations and agreed-upon goals. You may want to refer to the employee's latest performance appraisal. If the employee has personal problems, these can be dealt with on a case-by-case basis.

After each conversation, dictate a letter to the files giving the gist of the conversation. You may want to have the employee initial it so you have a record that the employee understands that he or she is not performing up to standards. If conversations do not achieve the desired result, you may want to write a warning memo.

There are several key things to remember in writing letters and memos that deal with personnel matters. Deal with facts (rather than opinions) as much as possible. Have an attorney check anything that has contractual implications—a statement of benefits, for example. And always adopt an objective rather than adversarial tone—people will simply respond better.

Announcement of Job Opening (7-01)

Company Name
Address
City, State Zip

To: All Staff

From: Donald J. Johnson

Date:

Subject: Opening for Secretary/Sales Assistant

As you know, Nina Kamchatka will be leaving us in two months to relocate to San Diego. Her position as Secretary/Sales Assistant will therefore be open. We always prefer to promote from within, and we welcome applications from anyone interested.

Duties include (but are not limited to):

- Providing secretarial support for Vice-President of Sales
- Typing all correspondence
- Managing extensive phone contact with clients
- Maintaining sales and records
- Making travel arrangements

Skills required are:

- Typing at 65 wpm
- Six-months' familiarity with PC and spreadsheet programs

Nina has offered to discuss her duties and the nature of her job with anyone who has an interest in succeeding her. Please call Joe Doddsworth in Personnel if you would like additional information.

- Announcing a job opening should be done in memo format.

- Use a positive tone and be very specific about the skills required.

- Saying that the list of duties is not complete covers you later on and avoids having the new hire saying "that's not my job."

Company Name
Address
City, State Zip

To: All Employees

From: William Winston

Date:

Subject: Recruiting New Employees

The unemployment rate in our area is now 3% and dropping. As a
result, we're having difficulty finding and recruiting new telemarketing
hires, despite the fact that our wages are above average and we offer
flexible hours for students and mothers.

Because we want the very best people available, we want to enlist your
help in finding people who are as qualified as you. We'll give you $100
for each person you recommend that we ultimately hire, and we'll give
you an additional $500 if that person stays with us for three months.
Remember that the people we want must have superb telephone skills
and an extremely responsible approach to working.

Please call me directly for further information (and please be sure
anyone you refer to us mentions your name as a referral).

- Your own employees are a valuable source of leads. Businesses live and die on the quality
of their people, and it's worthwhile to reward referrals.

Company Name
Address
City, State Zip

Date

Mr. Craig Stern
23 Dolphin Way
Port Washington, NY 11050

Dear Mr. Stern:

Thank you for sending your resume.

At this time, we do not foresee any branch manager openings with our firm during the next six months to one year. Generally, these positions are filled internally. No one can anticipate the future, though, and we'll gladly call you if we expand even more rapidly than anticipated.

Thank you for your interest in New Age. Please keep us in mind as you progress in your career.

Yours truly,

Walter Parker
Vice President, Sales

- Don't ignore an unsolicited resume even if you have no instant need for the person. There's always the future to consider.

- Consider your letter another opportunity to "sell" your firm and indicate that your firm is a good place at which to work.

Company Name
Address
City, State Zip

Date

Mr. Mark Canter
1650 Handler Drive
Fort Worth, TX 76125

Dear Mr. Canter:

I enjoyed talking with you on the phone Tuesday. We appreciate your promptness in sending along your resume, and, naturally, we give a great deal of weight to Phil Beckwith's recommendation.

As I mentioned on the phone, we expect to have openings for sales representatives in the spring. We will keep your resume on file and call you for an interview at that time.

If you do not hear from me by April 30, please call and check on the status of our hiring process.

Best,

Thomas H. Stanley
Personnel Manager

- Always respond immediately to job inquiries, even if you do not have an immediate opening. A job applicant is a potential member of your team and should be treated with courtesy.

- Provide an opportunity for the job seeker to re-establish contact, if appropriate. Leaving the ball in the job seeker's court will ensure that you aren't viewed as neglectful in the future.

Company Name
Address
City, State Zip

Date

Mr. Howard Fitzgibbons
567 Parakeet Way
Houston, TX 77034

Dear Mr. Fitzgibbons:

Thank you for taking the time to come in and fill out an application for the position of night store manager. Although we were certainly impressed with your qualifications, and the hours you were available were consistent with our requirements, I'm sorry to tell you that we'll have to put you on our waiting list.

While we currently do have a full roster of night managers, openings do occur from time to time. Please let us know if you change your address so that we may locate you if an opening does occur.

Sincerely,

Henry Carradine
Vice President, Personnel

- This letter is a bit more encouraging than a "we'll keep you on file" letter because it asks for notification of an address change, which is outside normal "form-letterese." It's always better to offer job seekers some hope (if it exists). It doesn't cost anything, and it leaves a very positive impression of your company.

Company Name
Address
City, State Zip

Date

Mr. Charles Plowright
150 Valentine's Lane
Old Brookville, NY 11511

Dear Mr. Plowright:

Mike Stamp tells me that you are interested in talking with financial planning firms like ours about the possibility of working as an associate with the expectation of ultimately being made partner. Mike speaks very highly of you, both as a solid person to work with and as a high producer with a substantial client base. We're very interested in both aspects of your experience.

Our firm has expanded rapidly in the past five years—we now have four partners and ten associates—and we have every expectation of continued growth as financial planning becomes more important to individuals and as our Long Island community grows.

We'd very much like to talk. Please call me at your earliest convenience.

Sincerely,

Thomas C. Calandra
Executive Vice President

- A letter to the person's home is a good way to approach someone who can't be or shouldn't be reached on the job. (Calling at home may be viewed as intrusive.)

- "Sell" your firm in the letter.

Company Name
Address
City, State Zip

1. Tell me about your present job.

2. Tell me how your boss and/or co-workers would describe you.

3. Describe your greatest work-related accomplishment within the last five years.

4. Describe your most frustrating work-related experience in the past five years and why it was so.

5. When given a new assignment or project, how do you approach it?

6. In what type of position are you most interested?

7. Do you prefer working with others or by yourself?

8. What led to your interest in our company?

- These questions should yield useful information about the applicant's strengths, weaknesses, working style, and self-perception. Good interviewers allow the applicant's own questions and responses to drive the interview.

- Do not ask questions that are either illegal (discrimination by race, creed, or sex) or highly personal.

Company Name
Address
City, State Zip

Date

Mr. Brian Poor
28 Trumbull Street
New Bedford, MA 02740

Dear Brian:

We were quite impressed with your qualifications, and after some consideration, we have decided that you are the ideal choice for the position of Unit Manager at Wesley Video Productions. Congratulations, and welcome aboard!

The terms are as we discussed in the interview. The salary is $30,000 a year. You'll have three weeks vacation per year and Blue Cross/Blue Shield health insurance. All employees at Wesley Video get five personal days and 10 sick days per year. We have a pension plan that you can sign up for after working at Wesley Video for one year.

We would like you to start on Monday, April 23. If you have any questions, please call us. If not, we'll see you on the 23rd!

Very truly yours,

Peter Vaughn
Vice President, Production

- Don't get into the specific responsibilities of the job. The point of this letter is to have a written record of the terms of employment. It's really a confirmation of previous discussions, so keep it simple and to the point.

Company Name
Address
City, State Zip

Date

Mr. Richard Pearle
41 Hallen Drive
Pace, FL 32570

Dear Mr. Pearle:

Thank you for responding to our job offer so promptly. We understand that there are some details to be worked out, but none of them appear to be insurmountable.

I spoke with the President of Kidsworks, Alan Weiss, and we both feel that we cannot increase the base salary we offered beyond $52,000 per annum. However, we can include a performance bonus of 15%, subject to review of both Mr. Weiss and myself. We will also include $5,000 to cover your relocation expenses.

If you have any further questions or comments, please call my office.

Sincerely,

Elaine Drile
Vice President

- Pretty self-explanatory. Keep things congenial because everybody will soon be working together, and you should therefore reduce the potential for bad blood developing.

- Make your offer and be sure to keep the lines of communication open.

Company Name
Address
City, State Zip

Date

Mr. Jason Clarides
P. O. Box 177
Sylvia, KS 42923

Dear Mr. Clarides:

It was a pleasure to meet with you last week in our offices at Senior Care, Inc. Your training in social work and business administration gives you a combination of skills that will be useful in any gerontology-related field.

As we discussed during the interview, Senior Care is looking for a person with at least five years of management experience in a residential facility for senior citizens. Because of your limited managerial experience, we are unable to offer you the position.

I wish you all the best for a successful career working on behalf of senior citizens.

Sincerely,

Carla Schultz
Vice President, Personnel

- Begin your letter by acknowledging one of the interviewee's areas of strength that you learned about during the interview.

- Let the applicant know why he or she doesn't meet your requirement by stating your unmet need.

- Close your letter with cordial good wishes for the future.

Company Name
Address
City, State Zip

Date

Mr. Frederick Hartland
56 Long Ridge Lane
Hartford, CT 06110

Dear Mr. Hartland:

I am sorry to tell you that, since we did not hear from you in response to our job offer, the offer expired as of last Friday.

I understood, when we spoke three weeks ago, that you were considering other opportunities, and we agreed that our job offer would be time-limited. I am, as you can imagine, personally disappointed that you won't be joining us as my Executive Assistant, but I hope that you will remember our conversations and consider Thomlinson Antique Auction Gallery if you decide to reevaluate your career in the future.

Best of luck in your new job.

Sincerely,

Allan J. Klein
Vice President

- Even if someone has been impolite (letting a job offer expire, rather than calling or writing, is quite rude), do not let your impatience be reflected in your tone. Something tragic may have happened, or the mail may have gone astray.

- Always keep the door open for future contacts.

Company Name
Address
City, State Zip

To: James Murdock

From: Timothy Nixon

Date:

Subject: Hours of Work

As we discussed in our meeting on October 10, it's important for you to reach the office on time. No one objects to an occasional slip. In fact, with the difficulties of commuting these days, being late once in a while is quite understandable.

Here's the problem, though. In the last month, even though we had already discussed the company's expectations at our October 10 meeting, you have been from 30-45 minutes late on seven (7) days, specifically October 14, 17, 18, 20, 26, 27, and November 1. This kind of performance is unacceptable—it sends me the message that you don't care about the job, and it certainly sets a bad example for your secretary, who is always here on time, even early most days.

There may be something that prevents you from getting to work on time. If there's anything I need to know, let's talk. However, you must improve your on-time performance to no more than one day late during the next month or I'll have to send you a formal warning which will be placed in your personnel file.

- It's only fair to tell employees when their performance is inadequate. Usually, you tell them first face-to-face. Then, if they don't improve, you should notify them in writing.

- Be specific about what you want improved and state a deadline. In serious cases, this becomes part of a written record to justify termination.

Company Name
Address
City, State Zip

To: Richard Candy

From: Bob Rolfe

Date:

Subject: Excessive Sick Days

In my memo of March 3, I stated that you had already used 10 sick days this year—the number of sick days allowable for the entire year. During March, you called in sick an additional three days— March 17, 18, and 21.

We value all our staff members, but we must warn you formally that any additional sick leave this year will be unpaid. Please schedule a meeting with me to discuss this problem as soon as you can.

- This memo reflects a personnel situation that has already deteriorated and may be unsalvageable. It represents a formal warning. The plea for a meeting is a last-ditch attempt to save the situation.

- Be specific as to the action expected and the time period involved.

Company Name
Address
City, State Zip

Date

Mr. Joseph P. Duffy
60 Sachem Street NW
Washington, D.C. 20332

Dear Joe:

As we discussed on Monday, the downturn in the market for industrial fans in the Washington region has led the company to close the regional office. As a consequence, your position has been eliminated.

To confirm our conversation, you will terminate your employment on June 22 and receive severance pay equal to three months' salary. The company will pay your medical insurance for the remainder of the year. In lieu of profit sharing for this year, you have agreed to accept a one-time payment of $5,000. Your retirement benefits will be retained by the company until we receive instructions from you.

Sincerely,

Thomas Sweet
Vice President, Personnel

Attachment

- Terminating an employee, for whatever reason, is a delicate subject and should be discussed first in person, then followed-up with a confirming letter like this one.

Company Name
Address
City, State Zip

Date

Mr. Melvin Jobs
President
Grove Water Distributors
40 Isleboro Walk
Augusta, ME 04330

Dear Mr. Jobs:

I'm delighted to respond to your request for a reference for Bonnie Bronson, who was our office manager for the past two years.

We were extremely disappointed to lose Ms. Bronson because of her relocation to Maine. She was almost entirely responsible for organizing the office systems here at Mechanical Systems, Inc. In short, she took us from an office in which we were constantly on a catch-up basis to one in which our systems for billing, collections, and personnel were sensible and controllable. Furthermore, her management skills were evident through her relations with our part-time clerical staff. She was totally responsible for hiring and training these three individuals, and a conversation with any of them reveals that she dealt with them fairly and professionally.

If you need an office manager who is responsible, is skilled, and has potential for advancement, you should hire Ms. Bronson.

Sincerely,

Melissa Anderson

- This is an easy letter to write—it's a rave review, and you can send a blind carbon copy to Ms. Bronson herself.

- Note, though, that the good reference is backed up with specific details.

Company Name
Address
City, State Zip

Date

To Whom It May Concern:

During the past two years, I have had the distinct pleasure of having Caryl Adams work for me at Bilcott Industries. As she leaves to accept new challenges, I welcome this opportunity to provide a recommendation on her behalf.

In my association with Caryl, she has been an integral part of the Operations Research Department as an Operations Analyst. Her work has been exemplary. She has provided timely, accurate, and insightful analyses to our clients across all industries.

Her writing and analytical skills are sharply honed. She is industrious and dedicated. Caryl's approach to her job can be characterized as truly professional. I wish her my very best as she seeks new frontiers.

Sincerely,

Phillip George
President

- When a good employee leaves for "greener pastures," it's not uncommon to be asked to write such a letter.

- To provide context, mention where, in what relationship, and for how long you knew the candidate.

- Stress the person's strong points, and how they might fit in with the individual's career objectives.

Company Name
Address
City, State Zip

Date

Ms. Sylvia Toth
Personnel Director
Scientific Investigations, Inc.
40 Washburn Street
Sandusky, OH 44870

Dear Ms. Toth:

We received your letter asking for a reference for Jane Howell. I have reviewed our personnel records.

Ms. Howell worked for Atlee Industries for just under two years. She started out as a receptionist and became a secretary for our Marketing division after one year. Her salary when she left was $19,200. She left Atlee because her husband had been relocated. Ms. Howell was well liked by her co-workers.

If you have any further questions, please call my office.

Sincerely,

Janet Birkowski
Vice President, Personnel

• Comments should be restricted to work-related matters. Personal criticisms should be avoided. You are being asked what kind of worker this person is, not whether you like him or her.

Company Name
Address
City, State Zip

Date

Mr. Stephen Montgomery
Institute of Management Research
2101 L Street NW
Washington, D.C. 20037

Dear Mr. Montgomery:

Edward Potts has given your name as a reference for an associate's
position with Toombs, Hardy and Foulkes. Would you provide for us
your impression of Mr. Potts' talents and strengths as a professional
and as a team player, as well as any other thoughts that you feel would
aid us in making a decision.

Thank you.

Sincerely,

Harvey Simpson
Partner

- Give the name of the person and the position for which he or she is being considered.

- Give an idea of the kind of information you want, while also soliciting any additional facts that might prove helpful.

Request for Verification of Employment (7-19)

Company Name
Address
City, State Zip

Date

Mr. Harold Ramones
Calhoun Trucking Company
270 Cottage Street
Springfield, MA 01104

Dear Mr. Ramones:

We wish to verify that Bryan Constantine (SS #021-36-8080) was employed by your company as a driver from December 2, 1983, to April 4, 1988. We are considering Bryan for a position as a driver and would like this and any other information you have regarding his value as an employee.

Thank you.

Sincerely,

Lloyd Daniels
Vice President, Personnel

- Give the candidate's full name (and social security number if you have it) as well as the period of employment on which you're checking.

- Take advantage of the opportunity to ask for additional information you might need.

Company Name
Address
City, State Zip

Date

Mr. Clarence Goodwin
Picnics Unlimited
55 Eastern Meadowlark Drive
Atlanta, GA 30305

Dear Mr. Goodwin:

You asked us to confirm certain information from Harley Stone's employment application in writing.

Harley Stone worked for Catering Around, a division of our firm, from June 1985 to July 1988. He began as a driver, a position he held for 6 months. For the rest of his employment period, he was a bartender and waiter. He left our company to move to Atlanta, where his wife had taken a new job. This information agrees with that given on Mr. Stone's application.

If we can help you in any other way, please call or write.

Sincerely,

Ann Richardson

- If you're asked to verify facts of employment, do just that and no more. Launching into unsolicited opinions may get you into trouble.

Company Name
Address
City, State Zip

To: All Employees

From: Hoyt Murdock, Human Resources Manager

Date:

Subject: Description of Expanded Health Insurance Coverage

Our department is constantly reviewing employee benefits to provide
improvements. Most recently, we focused on our psychological benefits
package in response to requests from employees and with a view to
general trends among other major regional employers.

As a result of our evaluation, we are pleased to announce that as of
June 30, the lifetime limit on reimbursements for in-patient psychiatric
treatment has been increased to $50,000. In addition, GHCP will now
reimburse out-patient psychological counseling at $40 per visit; annual
limits on out-patient visits have been increased to $1,000 per year. The
lifetime limit for out-patient psychological counseling has been
increased to $10,000.

These new benefits will be described in our annual benefits brochure,
but you may wish to keep a copy of this memo on file for reference.

- Benefits are important to employees, but the specifics may be ignored until the benefit is
  actually necessary. If you've made a major advance in benefit coverage, announcing it in a
  separate memo will encourage those concerned to pay attention and will give the personnel
  folks some welcome public relations help.

RESPONSIBILITIES OF A RETAIL CLERK

Retail Clerks in an Apple Pie Video Rental Store are primarily responsible for taking care of customers by receiving and renting films. Other duties may be assigned by the store manager.

Time Spent	Duties
75%	Handles customer requests in person and by telephone. Rents videos, receives returned videos. Completes paperwork for new memberships. Operates the store computer. Receives payment, makes change.
15%	Files returned videos. Returns display boxes to shelves. Keeps shelves orderly.
10%	Puts labels on promotional mailers. Dusts shelves. Receives shipments. Logs special requests. Checks drop box. Performs other duties as requested.

Skills Required

1. Must have good public relations skills.
2. Must be able to maintain the store's filing and shelving systems.
3. Must be able to learn and effectively operate the store computer.
4. Must be able to make change accurately.
5. Must be willing to perform other assigned duties.
6. Must be available and dependable for flexible scheduling of work hours, including holidays.
7. Must be able to work independently and without regular supervision.

Apple Pie Video Rental Stores, 2 Celluloid Square, Americus, GA 35291

• Time allotments help to explain both the nature of the work and the employer's priorities.

• Be sure to include special expectations in the job description, such as availability to work on holidays. This can deter the "but that's not in my job description!" blues for both employer and employee.

Summertime Concessions, Inc.
23 Sugar Mill Lane
Buhler, Kansas 49387

JOB DESCRIPTION

TITLE: Office Manager

GENERAL DESCRIPTION: This is a full-time position in which the person has responsibility for managing the office, handling assigned duties, supervising employees, and assisting the company president as needed. Because Summertime Concessions, Inc. is a small, family-owned business, the Office Manager has a broad range of duties. These vary from standard secretarial tasks to making sound judgment calls in the occasional absence of the president. The position answers to the company president.

SKILLS AND QUALIFICATIONS:
- Minimum of two-years experience as an office secretary with experience in supervising employees.
- Competence in use of the Macintosh computer for wordprocessing.
- Knowledge of food services and concessions management is highly desirable.
- Ability to work effectively with minimal supervision and to take initiative in problem-solving.
- Willingness to assist other office employees when needed and to perform other duties as required.
- Availability to work overtime to assist with inventory (usually one week per year).
- Ability to complete assigned workload satisfactorily.
- Ability to supervise and motivate employees effectively.

- A good job description is specific without being compulsively detailed. It should give the reader a clear idea of what the job entails and what is necessary to be successful at it.

- When writing a job description, think in terms of the qualities you desire in an employee (e.g., willingness to pitch in) as well as the skills required to get the job done.

Pygmalion Consultants, Inc.

PERFORMANCE APPRAISAL FORM

Use the reverse side if necessary

Date _____

Employee _____   Position _____

Evaluator _____   Position _____

COMPETENCIES/AREAS OF STRENGTH:

Brad, your skills as a training specialist and consultant are excellent. You are a very strong teacher and group facilitator. Your recent workshop for agoraphobics is a fine example of your abilities in this area, especially your ability to be sensitive to both individual and group needs.

I am pleased by your ability to research and design workshops and seminars. Your designs are practical, thorough, and suited to the knowledge level of the participants.

You have also been an asset to Pygmalion Consultants in your ability to network and generate referrals for the company. The increased business (and bonuses!) have made everyone happy.

CONCERNS/AREAS FOR IMPROVEMENT:

As we have discussed before, your tendency to produce results at the eleventh hour has been problematic. An example is the way several of the staff were forced to work overtime to finish the Golden Valley Public School Teachers project. Your expectation that the support staff can and will set aside their work at the last minute is unreasonable. As you know, good working relations between the staff and the consultants are a necessity. How can we work together to solve this problem?

Although you always dress neatly, your preference for casual dress in the office has become inappropriate. The company considers its image to be important both "at home" because of visiting clients and in public because of general professionalism. We expect you to wear business suits in and out of the office and to keep the tie tied and the sleeves buttoned.

- Make your evaluations specific. Back them up with examples.

- When evaluating undesirable performance, state clearly what you find unacceptable, why it is problematic, and what changes you expect the employee to make.

Summertime Concessions, Inc.

PERFORMANCE APPRAISAL FOR _____

This appraisal is based on the list of responsibilities, skills, and qualifications listed in the job description for an Office Manager. The evaluator should rate the employee in each category and use the adjacent space for explanatory comments.

Rating System
    1 = Needs improvement/Not adequate
    2 = Fair/Minimally adequate
    3 = Good/Adequate
    4 = Excellent/More than adequate

1. Competence in use of computer/word processer: 1 2 <u>3</u> 4
   Your skills have been steadily improving.

2. Knowledge of food service and concessions management: 1 2 3 <u>4</u>
   *What you didn't know when you started you've
   learned quickly!*

3. Ability to work effectively with minimal supervision: 1 2 <u>3</u> 4
   *Although you still need some coaching on the
   Macintosh, you do fine otherwise.*

4. Ability to take initiative in problem-solving: 1 2 <u>3</u> 4
   *I expect this will increase as you learn the business
   more thoroughly.*

5. Willingness to assist other employees: 1 <u>2</u> 3 4
   *Could use improvement here, especially when
   facing deadlines.*

6. Willingness to perform other duties as required: 1 2 3 <u>4</u>
   *It's good to know we can count on you to get the
   job done—whatever it is!*

7. Ability to complete assigned workload satisfactorily:　　1 2 <u>3</u> 4
   *Your work is high quality but is sometimes
   completed late (usually because you are a
   perfectionist!), so time management is an issue here.*

8. Ability to supervise and motivate employees effectively:　　1 2 <u>3</u> 4
   *My concern here relates to #5. Your supervision is
   generally good, but it's hard for you to stop what
   you're doing to help others during a crunch.*

<u>Additional Categories and Comments</u>

*Overall, we're very pleased with your work. You are dependable,
a hard worker, and able to manage efficiently several demanding
tasks at once.*

*Your work could be improved by better monitoring of office
expenditures to keep from going over budget again.*

*Another area of concern is your occasional tardiness. Although
you make up your time, it is important that you arrive promptly
at 8:30.*

---------------------------------   -------------------------------   ---------------
Signature of Evaluator　　　　　Position　　　　　　　　Date

I have read and discussed this performance appraisal with the
evaluator. My comments, if any, are on the reverse side.

---------------------------------------   --------------------------------
　　　Signature of Employee　　　　　　　　　Date

- A standardized form helps you to evaluate performance based on the actual job description. This style enables you to elaborate on your ratings.

- Leaving space for additional feedback allows you to include other points of praise or criticism and serves as an opener for discussion.

Company Name
Address
City, State Zip

Date

Mr. Grant Savage
40 Mayflower Street
Niagara Falls, NY 14304

Dear Grant:

I'm delighted to confirm your promotion to Director of Parts & Service. When we interviewed internal and external candidates for the position, your five years of loyal service and progressively more responsible positions with the company weighed heavily.

I understand you're planning to take two weeks vacation and assume your new position April 18. At that time, your salary will be $30,000 a year. Your benefits, which we discussed earlier, are described in the attached customized printout.

Since Parts & Service is a major profit center for our dealership, we're very pleased to have you in charge.

Sincerely,

John Brody

Enclosure

- Promotion letters are easy to write, especially since the promotion has already been discussed in person. Strive for a warm but not effusive tone.

- Make sure all details—salary, starting date—are clear.

Company Name
Address
City, State Zip

Date

Ms. Linda Wellington
45 Grand Avenue
New Haven, CT 06513

Dear Linda,

I'm pleased to tell you that your salary for next year, starting on the
anniversary day of your employment, will be increased 5% to reflect the
cost-of-living increase, plus an additional 8% merit increase based on
the achievements and increased skills we discussed at your appraisal
meeting. This brings your salary to $37,500 next year.

We're delighted to have you with us and look forward to another
productive year.

Best wishes,

Susan Makepeace
Vice President, Personnel

- Because salary issues are sensitive, these letters are usually sent home.

- Be very specific about the salary figures. Don't let the reader puzzle over the impact of the
  percentages.

Company Name
Address
City, State Zip

Date

Mr. Frank Peabody
Microchips Etc.
1345 Eglin Avenue
Dublin, OH 43017

Dear Frank:

Thought I'd drop you a note to let you know how well you handled the presentation to Datastar yesterday. I tried to get to you afterward, but you were in deep conversation with John Truman and I had to dash for the plane.

The presentation was great. You really zeroed in on their main issues— turnaround time and capabilities. Even more impressive was the way you handled the question and answer session. You were brief and to the point. You refused to argue with our always contentious client, Mr. Ackerman, and you brought everything to closure after you wrapped up the question and answer session. Keep this up and we'll be giving you more of these kinds of assignments.

Best,

Simon Schotts
Executive Vice President

- This should be a very informal, handwritten note—sent to an employee you don't see daily.

- People are far more motivated by sincere praise than by blame, and the remarks are most effective when they are very specific.

Managing Your Business 8

Despite the fact that most of us would prefer to spend all our time on the creative or income producing aspects of our businesses, the reality is that no business can run itself—that is, operate efficiently without coming to grips with the day-to-day logistics of carrying on operations.

Inquiry letters are vitally important because even though you may have adequate financial backing or a large departmental budget, even if you are noted for your technical competence, you still need information on *how to run your business*. Given the complexity of the modern business environment, you have a much better chance of getting the information you need if you put your request on paper and you ask the reader to reply in writing. People may give you a glib answer over the phone, but they'll think twice about misinforming you in writing. In addition, because it takes time to write, you can use these letters to separate those who truly want your business (and therefore are likely to give you good service) from those who take a lackadaisical approach to their customers.

To get the maximum benefit from inquiry letters, be very specific about the result you want from the interchange. Even when your intent is to buy something, don't waste the reader's time and your own by making a vague request. Think about what your needs are before you write. If you can, lay out the precise criteria you intend to use to make the purchase. If you simply cannot pay more than a certain amount of money, for example, telling the vendor what your limits are may forestall his all-too-human tendency to suggest more elaborate and pricier products or services than you can afford.

Inquiries and confirmations concerning travel arrangements and meetings must be very exact. Anyone who has ever found himself in an inadequately curtained meeting room at high noon with the wrong slide carousel for a 35-mm slide presentation can attest to this. Getting all logistical arrangements in writing can save endless time and aggravation. It is also only fair to hotel or rental service personnel, who may be juggling numerous requests and demands for the same facilities on the same day.

If asking for exactly what you want is half the battle, using the appropriate tone is the other half. People can be better judged by the way they treat subordinates and service people than by the way they treat their bosses. If you have any question about the way you come across when you communicate with others, have someone else read your correspondence and give you some feedback.

Company Name
Address
City, State Zip

Date

Mr. Dennis Stimson
River Development Association·
3084 U.S. 33 North
Benton Harbor, MI 49022

Dear Mr. Stimson:

We would like to renew our office lease for an additional two years. We are very pleased with the office and the maintenance of the building itself.

When we re-read our lease, we noted that there was no automatic renewal clause. We would be willing to increase the rent by 5%.

Please call and let us know if this is acceptable.

Best regards,

Noel Johnson
Managing Partner

- Usually, you can initiate a matter like this with a phone call. Landlords are notoriously difficult to reach, however, so a letter is justified, particularly if the relationship has been relatively good in the past. More importantly, a written record will help avoid future misunderstandings about financial arrangements. You do *not* want to write if you are in a hostile, confrontational mood.

Company Name
Address
City, State Zip

Date

Mr. James C. Jagoe
Custom Business Plans, Inc.
4322 Pendragon Boulevard
Rocklin, CA 95677

Dear Mr. Jagoe:

As I mentioned in our phone conversation, Kirk Specialty Products has expanded rapidly in the last year and now has 20 employees. We want to put together a comprehensive insurance plan for our employees and for the business. Three local firms have been asked to submit proposals.

Please consider the following possible types of coverage when structuring your proposal:

- Health insurance, including hospitalization and major medical.

- A SMP (Special Multi-Peril Policy) for on-premises liability.

- Surety bond that will cover both general employee honesty and our payroll people.

- An OLT (Owners, Landlords, and Tenants) policy for ourmachinery and other equipment.

- A Business Automobile policy for the company-owned cars driven by myself and our three sales representatives.

Please submit your proposal and quote as soon as possible. We want to make our decision on insurance coverage by the end of the month.

Sincerely,

John F. Kirk

- Shop around when planning a major expenditure.

- Be as specific as possible about your needs so you will be able to compare proposals easily.

- Insist on a written proposal. You want to decide, not be "sold." You can always talk later.

Company Name
Address
City, State Zip

Date

Faxright Corporation
30 Canner Park Road
Melville, NY 11746

Dear Faxright:

Our firm, with 20 professional consultants, is interested in purchasing a facsimile machine to communicate more quickly with our clients.

Our criteria are:

- lowest possible price
- ability to delay transmissions until lowest phone rate periods
- good resolution of both text and photographs
- minimum service problems, preferably with self-diagnostics system

Please send me written information on how well your line of fax machines meets these criteria. (We will not respond to phone calls unless we have written information.)

Sincerely,

Jane Redmond
Purchasing Department

- If you're seeking information, help the salespeople out by stating your criteria.

- Insisting on written information helps you screen vendors. Those who don't bother to respond in writing don't care enough to deserve your business.

Company Name
Address
City, State Zip

Date

Mr. Russell Puhl
Computertime, Inc.
191 San Marcos Avenue
Mill Valley, CA 94941

Dear Mr. Puhl:

We recently noted in the *Mill Valley News* "Business Talks" column that you offer consulting services to small businesses. We have a public relations firm, and we need help interconnecting our current systems. We have three Mac Pluses and a Laserwriter, plus two very old IBM PCs and a NEC Daisy Wheel printer.

We would like consulting help to decide whether we should (or could) network our various systems, whether we need to purchase some software to port data between the two systems, and what kind of software we need to support our substantial business in presentation visuals.

Please call us and let us know your background and hourly rates.

Sincerely,

Tom Robinson
Office Manager

- It's helpful to tell people where you heard of them.

- Make sure you tell the reader what you want help with in the first paragraph.

- Don't overlook asking for background information.

Company Name
Address
City, State Zip

Date

Mr. John P. Duke
Wheel-Duke Venture Capital
3288 Buena Vista Drive
Rocklin, CA 95677

Dear Mr. Duke:

George Welles tells me that your firm provides financing for start-up
ventures. Before I submit a formal application, I'd like to know in more
detail what types of situations you prefer, what kind of participation you
usually require, what time limits you generally stipulate, and your
collateral requirements.

I will call you on September 10 to discuss these issues.

I look forward to our conversation.

Sincerely,

Merle C. Davies
President

- In this kind of stiutation, writing should get you a bit further than a phone call since it's formal and shows serious intent.

- It's vital that you get the details requested. The more similar your financial request is to those that the firm has favored in the past, the more likely you are to get funding.

Company Name
Address
City, State Zip

Date

Mr. Cecil Tompkins
Westport Town Engineer
Westport Town Hall
Westport, CT 06880

Dear Mr. Tompkins:

During the last four months, the Town has undertaken various improvements related to the sewer installations in the Rockland Park area. During the course of these improvements, a landfill dike was constructed across the inlet that runs from the Sound to our property line.

My primary concern is that the dike has created a large area of trapped brackish water and mud between the dike and our property. The resulting stagnant pools are a nuisance that is both unsightly and unhealthy. Sewage drainage from several businesses is now trapped. This problem will continue until the final extension of the sewer line. Inquiries at your office last week indicate that this project may not be funded for some years.

We request, then, that the area between the dike and our property be filled to a sufficient height to eliminate the water/swamp problem. The attached map indicates the area of concern.

I would be pleased to accompany you, or someone from your department, on a site visit. If you prefer, please review the situation and let me know as soon as possible if my proposed solution is workable.

Sincerely,

James A. Sterling

Attachment

- Create a sense of government responsibility for the problem in the first paragraph.

- Offer a solution or alternate solutions.

Request to Employment Agency for Information (8-07)

Company Name
Address
City, State Zip

Date

Personnel Resources, Inc.
32 Newman Square, Suite 340
Stamford, CT 06497

Dear Personnel Resources Staff:

We've noted with interest the bulletins on secretarial and administrative help that you send us on a regular basis, and we would like to inquire about your method of operation and your fees. Specifically, we would like to know whether you charge a percentage of the person's salary or a flat fee. We would also be interested in your guarantee. If the person leaves after a month's employment, is the fee refundable?

We would very much appreciate receiving your brochure and a current client listing.

Sincerely,

Benjamin O. Whitney
Vice President, Personnel

- It's always helpful to tell people where you heard about their firm. It establishes a more personal relationship immediately.

- Ask for a representative client listing so you can do a check of their competence and the types of businesses served.

Company Name
Address
City, State Zip

Date

Ms. Rachel Dornfield, President
Public Relations Strategies, Inc.
251 West 57th Street
New York, NY 10107

Dear Ms. Dornfield:

We've very much enjoyed having your firm as tenants for the past two years and hope to continue the relationship. As you know, your lease ends August 31, and you have an option to renew for an additional two years with a 10% escalation in rent, as before.

Please call or write and let us know what you intend to do. We hope for a positive answer.

Sincerely,

Andrew T. Forge
Vice President

- If it's hard to reach someone by phone, a note may get his or her attention. But sending a letter by itself isn't enough. Make a note to call within a week or so as the mails can be unreliable.

Company Name
Address
City, State Zip

Date

Mr. George Haight
Vivian Development Corporation
200 First Avenue
Des Moines, IA 50322

Dear George:

I'm happy that we've cleared up the misunderstanding about our renovations to our office space at 60 Ferry Street.

To recap, we are not making any changes to the building that will affect the load bearing capabilities of the existing structure. As you can see from the attached plan provided by our contractor, all new walls are non-load-bearing, and we plan no demolition of existing partitions or walls.

As we discussed yesterday, these changes are within the provisions of our lease. I'm glad you agree that these renovations will significantly improve the space.

Sincerely,

F. Anthony Cipriano

Attachment

- If there's any possibility of misunderstanding, put it in writing. (If the details imply any contractual obligations, you'll probably want your attorney to look at the letter.)

- Make sure your tone is reasonably informal and neutral. An adversarial tone almost never serves your needs.

Company Name
Address
City, State Zip

Date

Chief Clerk
Superior Court
Judicial District
235 Church Street
New Haven, CT 06500

Dear Chief Clerk:

Ms. Jodie L. Forbes has been notified to appear in the state court on July 2 for jury duty. Ms. Forbes is the sole secretary/administrative assistant in Watley and Carling's three-person office, and she is essential to the operation of the business. This is our busiest season and we could not process our orders if Ms. Forbes were to serve at this time.

Please excuse her from jury duty.

Sincerely,

William Watley
President

- Serving on a jury is a civic duty, and no one should be excused unless there is real hardship. If the person is an essential employee, providing evidence of the hardship may help.

- In some states, where the obligation for jury service involves "one day or one trial," it's probable that only a medical excuse from a physician will get the person excused.

Executive Summary

The Concept House, Inc., an innovative desk-top publishing company, seeks $500,000 in venture capital to fund initial start-up costs and to acquire a database of high-quality conceptual graphics for executive presentations.

The current desk-top publishing market has five relatively large firms, but none of them provides conceptual graphics by top artists. The major problem is the antiquated retrieval system, which makes turnaround time excessively long. As a result, most executives hire outside artists at very high rates. The Concept House will create a database using only top artists by paying them top prices on a per use basis.

The Concept House's management team, T. L. Williams and Joseph Frey, are both experienced. Williams has created the top-selling conceptual graphics computer program in the industry; Frey is an award-winning artist with extensive connections. Frey's task is to sign artists to exclusive contracts.

Sales and marketing forecasts project that investors will have a significant profit within the first two years. The partners, who have invested a very substantial percentage of their personal assets, project that they will buy out the venture capitalist interest in Year 4.

The Concept House provides a much needed service in a growing market.

Full information on this opportunity is available from Kyle Benson, President, Benson Associates, 1400 Manorhaven Boulevard, Port Washington, NY 11050, who is representing The Concept House.

- The executive summary should provide enough information to "sell" the venture capitalist on the need to talk further, without giving everything away.

- Naturally, if you are representing yourself, you will give your own name and address.

Company Name
Address
City, State Zip

Date

Lowell Y. Isaacson
Isaacson Ventures
Staten Island Development Center
2760 Victory Boulevard
Staten Island, NY 10314

Dear Mr. Isaacson:

I've attached an executive summary of a business plan for The Concept House, Inc., Inc., an innovative presentation graphics development company whose principals are seeking $500,000 in venture capital for a start-up situation.

If the financing arrangements interest you, I would be happy to send you a complete business plan. Please write or call me. I look forward to talking with you soon.

Sincerely yours,

Kyle Benson
President

Attachment

- To save everyone's time, it's better to get someone's attention by sending an executive summary with a cover letter rather than sending the entire business plan. With this method, you can determine who is interested in the concept and the general financial arrangements, without letting everyone know your competitive secrets.

Company Name
Address
City, State Zip

Date

Norman M. Ladue
Ladue Legal Services, Suite 45
1200 Six Mile Road
Battle Creek, MI 49017

Dear Norm:

Thanks for answering my question the other day. I understand that there may be more to the issue than meets the eye, but I appreciate your giving me some sense of my legal obligations. If my informal negotiations aren't successful, I'll call you immediately to set up an appointment.

Again, thank you for helping me out. You know you can always count on me to serve as your "tax hotline."

Give my best to June.

Best wishes,

Rochelle K. Waters
CPA

- Professionals are in the business of charging for their expertise. Don't abuse a friendship by asking for detailed (and free) advice. In this situation, there is clearly reciprocity—the writer and the reader trade information and advice freely.

Company Name
Address
City, State Zip

Date

Mr. Torrance C. Wayne
Conference Facilities Manager
The Proxmire Inn
32 Gathering Hill Lane
Amana, IA 52203

Dear Mr. Wayne:

I enjoyed talking to you Tuesday. The Proxmire Inn does indeed have the facilities we require for our firm's quarterly planning meeting.

I'd like to confirm that we've agreed to book "the cottage," which includes a large meeting room for our entire department (25 people), as well as two smaller conference rooms for committee meetings (8-10 people each). The date we agreed on was June 25.

We need the following A/V equipment:

In the large meeting room:
An overhead projector and screen
A VCR and monitor

In each of the smaller rooms:
An overhead projector and screen
Two flip charts

The fee for the cottage will be $800, to include the A/V equipment and lunch. I will be calling June 5 to check on these arrangements. In the meantime, please send me a written confirmation.

Sincerely,

Horace Hawkins
Vice President, Marketing

- It doesn't hurt to treat hotel personnel as if they were human beings. If you did enjoy talking to them, say so.

- Conferences can be scuttled by insufficient attention to logistics. Put it in writing and get a written response. Then follow up with a phone call.

Company Name
Address
City, State Zip

Date

Manager
The Gathering
3642 Autumn Street
Santa Monica, CA 90405

Dear Manager:

Our firm, Bowden, Inc., had an offsite meeting at your facility on May 11. We were greeted by Gus Menzies when we arrived, and we found his assistance invaluable for the rest of the day. He checked on our needs frequently but unobtrusively, handled our crisis with the overhead projector (which we had supplied) with good humor and swiftness, and, all in all, gave us an enormous amount of confidence that our every need would be met.

Please thank him for us.

Sincerely,

Joseph C. Trowbridge
Vice President, Sales

• Good service should be noted, and writing to the manager shows your gratitude, provides tangible recognition of the person, and helps assure that your company will get good service in the future. (People complain of the decline in service while failing to recognize that the decline in customer courtesy has accelerated it.)

Company Name
Address
City, State Zip

Date

Mr. David R. Rivers
Manager
Trail Drive Inn
2 Whipoorwill Way
Boise, ID 83709

Dear Mr. Rivers:

I have stayed at the Trail Drive Inn every September, December, and May for over 7 years. In every instance, I have been more than pleased with the facility and service.

Last week, however, I was horrified to return to my room to find that the maid had discarded (and, it ultimately transpired, incinerated) an entire carton of confidential papers that I had left on the credenza in my room. I spoke to the front desk clerk, who kindly tore up my bill. Nevertheless, I wish to make sure this costly and personally embarrassing episode is not repeated. Please note in your records that on subsequent stays, my room is to be cleaned, but that nothing, including the contents of wastebaskets, is to be removed until I check out.

Sincerely,

Owen Willis

- If you're a steady customer, say so up front; it makes a difference.

- If you want something to happen, you'll have to ask for it. Giving a facility an opportunity to make good on a loss allows them to keep a valued customer and gives you a greater feeling of security. Writing to the hotel manager is a good way of ensuring that you'll get what you want.

Internal Communications 9

Written communications were once the major method of communicating internally. As management styles became more participative and less directive, however, internal communication tended to be more in the form of a quick "huddle" in the hall, a short meeting, or a phone call rather than the standard memo. Now, with the advent of people operating in widely dispersed locations, the written word is once again assuming more importance.

A well run business or department demands writing. Take agendas, for example. Agendas have an action bias—they not only stipulate what actions are required, they also specify who is responsible for taking action. The person who writes them, therefore, has a much greater chance of getting decisions implemented than someone who runs a meeting by the "seat of his pants."

Recommendations and reports. A memo that makes a recommendation saves everyone time by highlighting the reasons for the recommendation. Many decision makers actually think better when they have something in writing (these are the people who say "send me a memo so I can react to it"), and creating a cogent, logical argument on paper may be all you need to do to convince the reader.

The report is a dying breed. It used to be considered a "product," an end in itself, but more and more the product is the decision, the action, or the plan rather than a tome gathering dust on the shelf. Whether or not reports are produced depends on the decision maker—some decision makers want reports to reassure them that all the bases have been covered; some only want a presentation that shows (rather than tells) them that the recommendation is based on tight reasoning and extensive research. In any case, the decision maker usually reads the executive summary. Perhaps he or she will read *only* the executive summary, especially if the writer has high credibility and a "good news" message. The executive summaries included in this section follow all the rules. They attract the reader's attention by telling him or her why it's important to read on, and then they tell the main point and summarize the organization of the report itself. To write a lucid executive summary, you must have good organization. Otherwise, you'll find yourself writing things like this: "This report begins with an introduction (what else would it begin with?) and continues with an analysis of the problem...I then discuss..." That approach, which may sound frighteningly familiar, is deadly dull.

Policies and procedures. Great care should be taken with any written explanation—whether it is a new policy or procedure or a clarification of an existing policy—because staff members often feel threatened by change. Take the time to detail why a change has been made or why a clarification is required. This will reduce needless speculation (often erroneous) by employees, and will help them understand the reasoning behind company decisions.

Announcements. Managers tend to speed through the writing of announcements, but that's a mistake. Even if a decision has already been made, and a change is already in the works, treating the staff as if they were uninvolved is insulting. Most efficient managers consult the people affected before making any major change, to get their comments and suggestions, so announcements of new procedures are surprise-free; that is, they merely confirm what has already been agreed upon. Similarly, promotions and resignations should be announced first in staff meetings, with memos following in case people haven't heard the news directly. Once again, the purpose of writing it down in these cases is to solidify and make real to people news that is already "old."

If an executive or manager must impart bad news to the entire company, a written communication is essential. A memo dealing with difficult conditions should be direct and should say clearly what problems must be faced. If there are potential solutions, of if employee cooperation can help in specific ways, the details should be spelled out.

Company Name
Address
City, State Zip

To: All Sales Representatives

From: Thomas Lavel

Date:

Subject: Quarterly Meeting

In response to the feedback session at the last quarterly meeting, our fourth quarter meeting will be held offsite—at the Huckleberry River Inn in Blackthorn on January 30. I've enclosed a simplified map and an agenda. As usual, the meeting will start at 9 a.m. and end at 4 p.m. I look forward to seeing you there.

- Meeting notices should be complete, including references to who, what, when, and where. Enclosing a map is essential for offsite meetings, and an agenda is also vital.

- If you have responded to staff suggestions, make sure you point it out.

Company Name
Address
City, State Zip

Date:

Time: 10:00 a.m. to 11:30 a.m.

Location: Meeting Room A

Objective: Decide whether to increase in-house production capacity in printing

Attendees: Christopher Covale
Michael Endolf
Simone Martens
Jud Powers
Jillian Stabley
Heather White

Agenda Item	Purpose	Time	Presenter	Material To Be Read in Advance
Establish criteria for making decision	Consensus	15 mins.	—	—
Review 5-year production figures	Information	10 mins.	J.S.	Figures
Estimate long and short-term demands	Decision	20 mins.	S.M.	—
Review cost estimate	Information	15 mins.	J.P.	Estimates
Consider potential short-term use of excess capacity	Decision	20 mins.	C.C.	Estimates

• Always indicate your objective and plan of action to give participants a sense of comfort that their time won't be wasted.

• Assign tasks to people to make sure they are involved and prepared.

Company Name
Address
City, State Zip

To: Printing Capacity Committee

From: Michael Endolf

Date:

Subject: Assingments for Facility Addition Presentation

Action	Person Responsible	Completion Date
Develop new exhibits showing demand by sector.	J.P.	July 18
Create chart for senior management, showing best, worst, and most likely printing demand trends; support with text attachments.	H.W.	July 16
Gather cost estimate for 2,000 and 4,000 square foot print shop additions.	C.C.	July 16

Next meeting scheduled for July 21.

- When you reach agreement on an item requiring action, write out the action and identify the person responsible.

- Distribute assignments as soon as possible after the meeting so those concerned can be aware of everyone's tasks and will know where to direct their own input.

Company Name
Address
City, State Zip

To: Cyril Schiller, President

From: Dolores Ofner

Date:

Subject: Media Strategy for Sunday Openings

At our February 20 meeting, we decided to open all suburban branches of the bank on Sundays in order to serve our existing customers better and to attract new accounts. I've met with Stiller and Orlando, our advertising agency, and they suggest a 12-week advertising campaign, using newspapers as the umbrella media.

In brief, they recommend the following:

Newspapers. Place one full-page ad each week in the four regional weekly newspapers for the first four weeks of the campaign. Run a half page each week in the two urban newspapers during the same period. To sustain awareness of the Sunday opening, a third, smaller ad should run in all newspapers for the remaining eight weeks.

Statement Stuffers. Supplement the newspaper ads with 70,000 statement stuffers to reach existing bank customers. The stuffers will use the same creative theme as the newspaper ads and will also be available as "take ones" in each branch office.

Cyril Schiller   -2-   Date

Drive-In Window and Lobby Posters. Place color posters at drive-in windows and lobby entrances at each of the branches.

Outdoor Advertising. Change the copy on our 24 billboards and put up a new billboard sign advertising the Sunday opening on 16 additional billboards. (See attached example.)

So far, S & O has not provided the specific reasoning behind their strategy. I feel strongly that we should not go ahead with this plan until they provide the back-up. Neither you nor I have enough expertise to evaluate their recommendations without it. In addition, I have told them that they must provide a budget as soon as possible.

Attachment

- Remind the reader of the reason for the memo—always a good idea.

- Highlight the main points with headings.

- Outline clearly the next steps to be taken.

Company Name
Address
City, State Zip

To: Brody Newhouse

From: Gus Marwick

Date:

Subject: Word Processing Work-flow

Thank you again for your recent suggestion about reorganizing the work flow in the word-processing department. We had a meeting with the people concerned last week, and they enthusiastically accepted your idea for assigning individual word processing operators to specific departments so that the operators can become familiar with the dictating styles of the individual managers and the technical subject matter. Naturally, we'll reassess the new system after a month or so to see how it's working, but we expect that it will be a great improvement over our current system, which has been the source of endless complaints.

John Harvey and I discussed this improvement in a recent meeting, and he wanted to make sure I thanked you for him as well.

- A steady flow of suggestions and recommendations is vital to a well-run business.

- Encourage communication by responding promptly, telling the specifics of the implementation, and making sure the word gets to higher-ups in the firm.

Company Name
Address
City, State Zip

To: All Staff Members

From: James R. Powers

Date:

Subject: Community Campaign

We have always had a proud tradition of supporting the Community Campaign, that excellent organization that helps us to extend a helping hand to the needy in our community.

Soon, you will have the opportunity to share in this fine tradition, once again, through your support of our annual Community Campaign.

By giving just one hour's pay each month, through payroll deduction, you ensure that the health and human care needs of our communities are met the whole year.

I urge you to join me in contributing to the Community Campaign so that together we may help improve the quality of life for everyone.

- Usually, the organizing institution provides boilerplate letters. Try to personalize them if possible.

- Make it easy by offering payroll deductions.

Company Name
Address
City, State Zip

To: Senior Management

From: Hal Wellington

Date:

Subject: Mid-point Progress Report—Marmot River Plant

As I reported last month, changing the coating of the steam lines to a zinc base, while worthwhile in terms of reduced cost, has caused us to slip the schedule by two months. We have had additional problems in the last month. Because of an early freeze, we were not able to break ground for the laboratory addition. We estimate that this setback will cost us six months for that part of the project. Because of the increased time involved, we will incur additional labor costs. We will therefore be over budget by approximately $56,000.

Impact of the early freeze confined to laboratory addition. No one could have anticipated the severity of the October 20 freeze, the worst in 25 years. The schedule, as outlined in our original proposal and as revised last month, was predicated on more normal temperatures. Naturally, this affects only the laboratory addition. Renovations to the main plant itself, where we have already "closed the envelope," or made the building weather-tight, will progress on the schedule we set forth last month.

Renovations to main plant close to revised schedule. We have completed the new flooring and all major rewiring. We have also replaced all light fixtures. This month we will be testing the flooring's ability to bear the new equipment. (All equipment was delivered on schedule. It has been stored in the yard for the past month under weather-proof sheathing.)

- Executive summaries for progress reports may be in the form of transmittal letters, memos (like this one), or individual pages after the title page.

- Use action headings (statements of significance) rather than generic headings (work completed, cost, conclusion) to make your points. If you're not on schedule, say so, and say why, without assigning blame or whining.

Executive Summary

J. M. Finnerty Corporation has had a contractual agreement with the Leveland County Commission on Human Rights since l986. This year's goal under the agreement was to fill 15% of the Corporation's middle-management positions with minorities and 35% with females, through either promotion or external search. Unfortunately, we have been unsuccessful thus far. Only 7% of our middle-management positions are held by minorities, 16% by women. If the corporation fails to meet these goals in the next 10-month period, the ensuing litigation could represent a cost of a minimum of $95,000, even if arbitration is possible in some instances.

We have contacted Herman K. Fanton, a consultant skilled in training management in minority recruiting practices, and he is willing to help us institute a new program that will:

- provide intensive training for each manager with hiring responsibility

- institute new skills training programs to encourage promotion from within

- evaluate progress at each step

Rationale and technical back-up (including consultant's proposal, graph detailing minority and female recruitment, and table of median legal costs in similar cases) are attached.

- Executive summaries for final reports come after the title page of the report and so require no heading but the title.

- State why the report is important and highlight its organization through the use of bullets. If the writer has high credibility, and if the reader finds the message convincing, agreement could be reached on the basis of the summary.

Company Name
Address
City, State Zip

To: Bob Pickett

From: Sylvia Presser

Date:

Subject: Lateness of Promotional Materials for Schweitzer's Soda

We've had a terrible time getting the printer to stick to the delivery schedule on the Schweitzer's Soda posters. I believe it is still possible to meet the deadline for delivery to the distributors, but it's going to be close.

There are two reasons for the delay. We were set back almost a full week when we discovered errors in the artwork. These mistakes should have been caught by my staff. We are going to change some procedures to prevent this from happening in the future.

The second problem is that we increased the printing order by over 50% at the client's request. The printer couldn't handle it, and it was too late to find another. We found another shop to augment the first, but we were already behind.

As I said, I think we will still make the deadline of June 5, but it's going to take some serious babysitting.

- Admit any errors or misjudgments on your part, but don't grovel. Take responsibility, and use straightforward, non-evasive language.

- Give the whole story. Often your boss must report to his boss, and he/she needs all the facts.

Company Name
Address
City, State Zip

To: Monica R. Tolman

From: Henry Dumont

Date:

Subject: System 10 Upgrade

I recommend we purchase an IBM 4420-H12 disk drive to address the storage capacity problem we now have with System 10.

Purchasing this unit will allow us to:

- add the storage capacity we need to complete projects now underway
- upgrade System 10 cost-effectively

Add Storage Capacity

The IBM 4420-H12 will provide 700 megabytes of auxiliary storage to System 10. It will eliminate our current critical capacity problem and allow us to move forward with our plan to provide additional system functions.

Upgrade Cost-effectively

The IBM 4420-H12, at $13,000, is the least expensive option for meeting our needs and avoids having to upgrade the entire system now. The two other units we have considered, the 3840-A12 and the 4420-H13, cost $41,000 and $26,000, respectively. Upgrading the entire System 10 now would cost over $50,000. Although the entire system will have to be upgraded eventually, I do not see sufficient reason to do so now.

The IBM 4420-H12 clearly suits our needs best. With your authorization, we can move ahead on purchasing and installing this unit.

- Lay out your specific recommendation up front and let the reader know why it's important.

- Clearly state the benefits of your recommendation.

- Be sure to end by restating your recommendation and telling the reader what needs to be done next.

Company Name
Address
City, State Zip

To: Investment Committee

From: John Lerue

Date:

Subject: Budget Finance Loan

At its next meeting, the Committee must decide whether to approve the purchase of $1.2 million of convertible debentures in Budget Finance Corporation, a financial services company, headed by George Ephram, that buys commercial paper from retailers in low-income neighborhoods. I recommend that we approve this purchase: It both meets our financial criteria and advances us toward our advertised goal of participating in the revitalization of low-income areas.

Financial Criteria

- Budget Finance should be able to make payments on schedule. The anticipated increase in business seems reasonable, given Budget's strong management and projected market growth.

    1. Budget's program should attract retailers and overcome the industry's traditional problems—shoddy merchandise, inadequate follow-up on defaults, and poor selection of potential customers.

    2. In addition, the bilingual partner and employees should attract new business in the Spanish-speaking community.

    3. Budget's experienced management, innovative systems, and training and computer programs, combined with a growing

economy, should easily provide Budget with the cash flow necessary to repay its debt to the bank.

Minority Community

- This loan will be a visible symbol of the bank's commitment to helping low-income areas.

    1. Budget is involved in almost every neighborhood in which we have a branch (see Exhibit 1).

    2. Joint advertising, both print and TV, will reinforce this tie.

    3. Acquisition of convertible debentures will demonstrate the bank's interest in participating in the ownership of local business.

    4. Budget's training programs and the loan will have a ripple effect: Budget will channel the bank's funds to retailers, indirectly contributing to their increased sales.

Attachments

- Memos recommending a course of action should have a very tight argument. Here the investment committee clearly cares about the financial issue—and about aiding the minority community.

- Use of bullets and numbered points help readers to absorb the major points quickly.

Company Name
Address
City, State Zip

To: All Staff

From: Len Fireman, President

Date:

Subject: Media Policy

Our policy for dealing with the media is to respond quickly and politely. Do not refuse to speak to media representatives or fail to return their phone calls. News is only news for a very short time, and the media must print or broadcast something. It's better if that something comes directly from a spokesperson for our company.

In general, it is best to refer media calls to me. I'm trained to deal with the media, and individual reporters are likely to prefer dealing with me in any case. If I am not available, Nancy Anne Hart, my administrative assistant, will know whom to call.

If no one is available and you must talk with a media representative, be sure that you do not give him or her misleading or incomplete information. Do not provide any information that could be construed as proprietary or personal. Do not give opinions—only factual information. If you do not know the answer to a question, say so. Never speculate. Your speculation is likely to be printed as a fact.

- Dealing with the media can be very stressful for people. Give the staff the names of company spokespersons to call, plus guidelines for dealing with media representatives that will ensure minimum strain.

Company Name
Address
City, State Zip

To: Clara Winstead

From: Bowman Steele

Date:

Subject: Changing Holiday Policy

We recommend changing the firm's holiday policy from 10 fixed
holidays to 7 fixed holidays (those indicated with an asterisk) and 3
"floaters":

> Day before New Year's
> New Year's*
> Good Friday
> Memorial Day*
> July Fourth*
> Labor Day*
> Thanksgiving*
> Day after Thanksgiving*
> Day before Christmas
> Christmas*

Our employees have asked for this change because the days before
New Year's and Christmas sometimes fall on a Saturday or Sunday
and because Good Friday has no significance for some of them.

We feel we should respond positively to their request as long as there is
adequate coverage assured in the office on "floating holidays." If you
agree with this change, please initial on the bottom and return this
memo to me. I'll take care of the rest.

- Make the nature of the change clear by stating what exists as well as what you recommend.

- Make it easy for the decision-maker to respond by giving your reasons and saying "initial this." The easier you make it, the more likely you'll be to get what you want.

Company Name
Address
City, State Zip

To: All Staff

From: Paul Pleasant

Date:

Subject: New File Back-up Procedures

For several years, we've survived quite nicely with a rather haphazard procedure for backing up our file disks. As the company has grown, however, we have been having problems. For example, people take the disks home to work on them, and other members of the staff cannot find copies. Furthermore, our insurance representative has pointed out that should we have a fire, our mailing lists and other proprietary data disks would be lost, and we would find it extremely difficult to reconstruct them.

As a result, we have instituted a new policy:

- Anyone using a disk must make a back-up copy. Back-up copies should be updated every Friday afternoon.

- Anyone who takes a data disk home must leave a copy in the office.

- Every two weeks, Hilary Newsome will take the essential data disks to the company's safe-deposit box. At that time, she will retrieve the old copies of the data disks for reuse. Program disks are already in the safe-deposit box. If any new programs are purchased, they must be taken to the safe deposit box on the next trip. If there should be any problem with initiating this policy, please contact me.

- Make sure everyone knows why the procedures are being implemented.

- Be very specific about *who*, *what*, *where*, and *when*. Assigning tasks and responsibilities by name is very helpful.

Company Name
Address
City, State Zip

To: All Staff

From: Eugene Robards

Date:

Subject: Lloyd Reed

I'm pleased to announce that Lloyd Reed has been made a principal in our firm. Lloyd has been with Robards, Robards, and Tolsory for five years. Previously he was Director, Human Resources, for Weaver Industries, with responsibilities encompassing diverse manufacturing operations, including international operations in the Far East.

A broadly experienced personnel executive, Lloyd spent ten years with Wellfleet, Inc. in a variety of personnel positions with emphasis in organization planning, executive selection, management development, and labor relations.

Lloyd is currently President of the Arthritis Foundation of Whittier, and a member of the Executive Committee of the Human Resources Research Association. Previously he served as a Director for the Whittier United Way.

- Business career information, both in the company and elsewhere, reinforces the individual's professional expertise.

- Non-business background information on the individual provides the human touch.

Company Name
Address
City, State Zip

To: All Staff

From: T. R. Kellogg

Date:

Subject: Sam Griffith's Departure

Sam Griffith, Vice-President of Product Marketing, has resigned to start his own marketing consulting firm, Griffith & Associates, in Phoenix. We are sorry to see Sam leave and will miss his sharp, incisive wit, but wish him the best in his new venture.

Those who wish to give Sam a proper send-off are invited for wine and cheese in the 3rd floor conference room on Friday the 23rd at 4 p.m.

- Say what the departing employee will be doing (if he's joining a competitor, you can merely say he's "leaving to join another firm").

- Mention some positive aspect of the person that you will miss.

Company Name
Address
City, State Zip

To: All Staff

From: T. G. Kellogg

Date:

Subject: Loss of Business

I am very sorry to announce that Southeastern Telecommunications, Inc., our largest customer, has decided not to renew its contract with us to supply computer maintenance services. More than 30% of our business was with Southeastern, so the loss of the contract will substantially diminish our operating revenues.

We expect to know the full impact of the contract loss within 30 days. Within that period we will learn whether contract negotiations with several potential customers, which would replace half of the Southeastern revenues, have been successful. I will keep everyone informed as events develop.

Because of the problems we will experience over the next few months, the company has furloughed six service technicians and three home office personnel. Jack Wiggins, Marketing Vice President, has left the company. No further reductions in staff are anticipated.

Our company has grown fast and established an enviable record in its 12-year history. I know that everyone will pull together in the next few months to help us get back on track.

- Be direct about bad news and state plainly its impact—on the company and employees.

- Outline what the company is doing to solve the problems and appeal for cooperation.

- Promise to keep the staff informed—and do so.

Company Name
Address
City, State Zip

To: All Staff

From: Bob Lee

Date:

Subject: Office Move

As you all know, we recently lost the Hechlind Lawn Maintenance and Landscaping account. Hechlind represented over 28% of our annual business, and we're doing everything we can to replace their account by soliciting new clients. In the meantime, however, we'll need to cut overhead costs in every way possible.

Our move to 46 Quinnipiac Place has been postponed indefinitely, and we'll have to endure our overcrowded conditions for a longer period of time. We hope we can make this situation more bearable by adjusting sales representatives' schedules. Clearly, however, we need to discuss contingency plans. I've called a staff meeting for next Monday, to discuss everyone's concerns and answer questions. In the meantime, please call me if you have any questions.

- Make sure people learn the bad news (that you lost the contract) from a company representative, not outside suppliers.

- Set up a meeting to discuss the implications as soon as possible.

- Make any explanation straightforward. Skip convoluted phrasing. People will think they are being conned.

Company Name
Address
City, State Zip

To: All Staff

From: Michelle Voss, Public Affairs

Date:

Subject: Policy Regarding Contacts with News Media

Because of the recent gas leak and explosion at our plant in
Marlborough, some of you have been approached by the local press to
talk about working conditions. I felt it was a good time to reiterate our
policy regarding such matters.

Our policy is simple. All contacts and queries will be referred either
to my office or to the office of the President. No one is to speak for the
company, or speak as an employee of United Manufacturing, except for
myself or Mr. Greenberg. This includes all "off the record" inquiries.

We want to emphasize that we do not wish to cover anything up. But
it is important, especially when there is the threat of lawsuits, that the
company speak with a single voice. We will continue to cooperate with
the authorities on this matter, and we feel that it is important that we all
do our jobs as effectively as we can. We believe that this policy makes
everyone's life easier.

If you have any questions, you may reach me at ext. 500.

- The policy stated in this memo is pretty standard. While it is quite restrictive, it's important
  not to come on too strong. Be forceful and to the point. Avoid spelling out sanctions.

- Be sure to say that this policy is for everyone's benefit, state the reason for your concern, and
  give people an opportunity to ask you questions.

Business Forms 10

How business documents look, particularly those sent outside the company, is as important to successful communications as their contents. This section provides styles for the major kinds of documents.

In addition to using the proper formatting, attention should be paid to the other physical aspects of business writing. You should use high-quality stationery, typing should always be neat, and spelling should always be checked (particularly the name of the reader).

Forms should be readable and simple to follow. The "plain English" movement has done a great deal to simplify forms, through appropriate use of white space (margins, space between paragraphs) and headings. Using a readable type face and resisting the temptation to mix fonts or to overuse italics or bold face also help ensure readability.

Company Name
Address
City, State Zip

quadruple space

To:
    double space
From:
    double space
Date:
    double space
Subject:
    triple space

First paragraph, body of the memo begins. (This is always single spaced with the paragraphs starting at the left margin.)
    double space
Next paragraph
    double space
Last paragraph
    double space.
Writer's initials (uppercase): typist's initials (lowercase)

CHAPTER TITLES

Chapter titles are set in all caps and centered on the page.

Section Headings

Section headings are also centered. They are upper case and lower case and underlined. You should have at least two heads at every level of subdivision.

Section Subheadings

Underlined subheadings, flush left, head each subdivision.

- If you are going to divide a subsection further, you may do so by using bullets or some similar mark of distinction. These sections should be indented.

- This is a popular format. You should also include an Executive Summary, a one-page summary of the entire report.

Company Name
Address
City, State Zip

Date:

Time:

Location:

Objective:

Attendees:

Agenda Item	Purpose	Time	Presenter	Material to Be Read in Advance

- A meeting's objectives should be clearly and precisely stated so participants will focus on the issues.

- Agenda items should start with broad topics and narrow toward the decision; stating the time for each item will force concentration.

Title
triple space

I. FIRST ORDER DIVISION—ALL CAPITALS
double space
   A. Second Order Division—First Letter Of Each Word Is Capitalized
      1. Third order division—Only first letter is capitalized
      2. Note that each division and subdivision is indented 4 spaces from the heading superior to it
         a. Fourth order division
         b. If you have an a, you must have a b
double space
II. IF YOU HAVE A 1, YOU MUST HAVE A 2

   A. _____
      1. _____
         a. _____
         b. _____
      2. _____
   B. _____
      1. _____
      2. _____

Company Name
Address
City, State Zip

Name of employee: _____   Department: _____

Performance Appraisal

Performance evaluation criteria

	Excellent	Very good	Good	Satisfactory	Needs Improvement
Quality of work					
Production output (quantity)					
Reliability (attendance, consistency of effort)					
Attitude (acceptance of direction)					
Interpersonal skills (communication)					
Knowledge of job					
Office skills (if applicable)					
Initiative (ability to work without supervision)					

Comments:

_____

_____

_____

Action steps: _____

Overall rating   <u>Excellent</u> <u>Very good</u> <u>Good</u> <u>Satisfactory</u> <u>Needs Improvement</u>

Evaluated by: _____

Employee signature: _____

Date: _____

- This form provides a place for free-form commentary as well as forcing "scoring." It should provide a starting point for discussion, not a substitute for it, and will help the evaluator to view the employee objectively.

- Fill out the action-steps section only after consultation with the employee.

Employment Application (10-06)

Company Name
Address
City, State Zip

Name: _____ Social Security Number: _____

Address: _____ Phone Number: _____

EMPLOYMENT

List all periods of employment, starting with the most recent.

	From	To
Company: _____	_____	_____
Address: _____		
Supervisor: _____		
Company: _____	_____	_____
Address: _____		
Supervisor: _____		

(If you need more space, attach another sheet or your resume.)

EDUCATION

	From	To	Degrees Obtained
High School: _____	_____	_____	_____
College or University: _____	_____	_____	_____

Other educational training, including trade, business, or military

_____

_____

REFERENCES

Please provide names of three people who are familiar with your qualifications. We will be calling or writing them so they must be those you want us to contact.

	Name	Address and Phone No.	Position
1.	_____	_____	_____
2.	_____	_____	_____
3.	_____	_____	_____

What else would you like to tell us? Please comment on anything about you—skills, work you have done, goals you have—anything we cannot tell from looking at your application (use the back of this sheet if necessary).

_____

_____

_____

I authorize the company to obtain information from any person named above, and I release all concerned from any liability in connection with obtaining and releasing such information.

_____
Applicant's Signature   Date

- Some firms ask everyone to fill out an application because it's easier to discern gaps or inconsistencies on an application than it is on a resume.

- This application is relatively simple, but it does allow for free-form comment. The tone of the questions is friendly rather than intimidating, a good reflection on your firm.

Company Name
Balance Sheet
December 31, Year

Assets

Cash and short term investments	$XXX
Accounts receivable, less allowance for bad debts of $XXX	XXX
Prepaid expenses	XXX
Furniture and fixtures, less accumulated depreciation of $XXX	XXX
Leasehold improvements, less accumulated amortization of $XXX	XXX
Other assets	XXX
Total assets	$XXX

Liabilities and Shareholders' Equity

Accounts payable	$XXX
Notes payable to banks	XXX
Income taxes payable	XXX
Other liabilities	XXX
Total liabilities	$XXX
Stockholders' equity:	
Common stock, $XX par value	$XXX
Amount in excess of par value	XXX
Retained earnings	XXX
Stockholders' equity	$XXX
Total liabilities and stockholders' equity	$XXX

- A Balance Sheet is a "snapshot" of your company's assets and liabilities as of a specific point in time, usually at the end of your financial year.

Company Name
Balance Sheet
December 31, Year

Assets

Cash and short term investments	$XXX
Accounts receivable, less allowance for	
bad debts of $XXX	XXX
Inventories	XXX
Prepaid expenses	XXX
Property, plant and equipment, less	
accumulated depreciation and	
amortization of $XXX	XXX
Other assets	XXX
Total assets	$XXX

Liabilities and Shareholders' Equity

Accounts payable	$XXX
Notes payable to banks	XXX
Accrued expenses	XXX
Income taxes payable	XXX
Other liabilities	XXX
Total liabilities	$XXX
Stockholders' equity:	
Common stock, $XX par value	$XXX
Amount in excess of par value	XXX
Retained earnings	XXX
Stockholders' equity	$XXX
Total liabilities and stockholders'	
equity	$XXX

- A Balance Sheet is a "snapshot" of your company's assets and liabilities as of a specific point in time, usually at the end of your financial year.

Company Name
Income Statement
For the Year Ending December 31, Year

Revenue

Service income	$XXX	
Interest and other income	XXX	
Total revenues		$XXX

Expenses

Salaries and benefits	$XXX	
Rent	XXX	
Utilities	XXX	
Interest	XXX	
Depreciation and amortization	XXX	
Bad debts	XXX	
Other expenses	XXX	
Total expenses		XXX
Income before taxes		XXX
Provision for income taxes		(XXX)
Net income		$XXX

- An Income Statement, also called Statement of Profit and Loss, summarizes revenue and expenses for a given period, usually one year, and reports the profit and loss from operations.

Company Name
Income Statement
For the Year Ending December 31, Year

Gross sales	$XXX	
Less: Sales returns, allowances and discounts	XXX	
Net sales		$XXX
Cost of goods sold	$XXX	
Sales salaries	XXX	
Advertising	XXX	
Depreciation and amortization	XXX	
Office salaries	XXX	
Bad debts	XXX	
Other expenses	XXX	
Total expenses		XXX
Net operating income		XXX
Other revenue and expense items:		
Interest and dividend income		XXX
Net income before income taxes		XXX
Provision for income taxes		(XXX)
Net income		$XXX

- An Income Statement, also called Statement of Profit and Loss, summarizes revenue and expenses for a given period, usually one year, and reports the profit and loss from operations.

Company Name
Address
City, State Zip
1 to 12 blank lines depending on length of letter (for shorter
letters leave more blank lines)
Date
1 to 12 blank lines depending on length of letter (for shorter
letters leave more blank lines)
Person's name
Title
Company name
Street address
City, State Zip
double space
Dear (salutation):
double space
First paragraph, body of the letter begins. (This is always single spaced
with the paragraphs starting at the left margin.)
double space
Next paragraph
double space
Last paragraph
double space
Sincerely yours,
quadruple space

Typed name
Title
double space
Writer's initials (uppercase): typist's initials (lowercase)
double space
Enclosure (if needed)

6 blank lines from top of page
Name of person who is receiving letter
Page 2
Date
    triple space

This is how you set up the second page of a letter in Full Block Style. All paragraphs begin at the left.
    double space
Next paragraph
    double space
Last paragraph
    double space
Sincerely yours,
    quadruple space

Typed name
Title
    double space
Writer's initials (uppercase): typist's initials (lowercase)
    double space
Enclosure (if needed)

Company Name
Address
City, State Zip

1 to 12 blank lines depending on length of letter (for shorter letters leave more blank lines)

Date

1 to 12 blank lines depending on length of letter (for shorter letters leave more blank lines)

Person's name
Title
Company name
Street address
City, State Zip
double space
Dear (salutation):
double space
First paragraph, body of the letter begins. (This is always single spaced with the paragraphs starting at the left margin or indented 5 spaces.)
double space
Next paragraph
double space
Last paragraph
double space

Sincerely yours,
quadruple space

Typed name
Title
double space
Writer's initials (uppercase): typist's initials (lowercase)
double space
Enclosure (if needed)

6 blank lines from top of page

Name of recipient   -2-   Date

triple space

This is how you set up the second page of a letter in Modified Block
Style. Remember that you can start paragraphs at the left margin or
indent 5 spaces.

double space

Sincerely yours,

quadruple space

Typed Name
Title

double space

Writer's initials (uppercase): typist's initials (lowercase)

double space

Enclosure (if needed)

Company Name
Address
City, State Zip

Date

Company Name
Address
City, State Zip

INVOICE

Basic fee .... $

Other itemized expenses .... $

Total: $

Invoice is payable upon receipt.

Please make check payable to: Company Name
Address
City, State Zip

- This form should satisfy accounting departments because it provides a description of the basic service and allows for extra expenses.

- There's no need to include the "Please make check payable to" unless it's different from the letterhead.

- Be sure to include when payment is due.

Company Name
Address
City, State Zip

INVOICE

Date   Number

Order #:
P.O. #:
Cust. #:
Terms:

SOLD TO: SHIP TO:

<u>ITEM#</u>   <u>DESCRIPTION</u>   <u>QTY.</u>   <u>UNIT PRICE</u>   <u>EXT. PRICE</u>

Sale Amount: $
Discount: $
Tax: $
<u>Freight:</u>   <u>$</u>

Total Sale: $

The Withey/Beatson Insurance Agency

cordially invites you to attend

their Christmas Open House

Tuesday, December 21, Year

6:00 - 8:00 p.m.

810 High Street

East Haven, Connecticut

R.S.V.P. by December 19
(203) 624-0728

- If you choose a formal typeface, the invitation will look even more impressive.

- Include all details on time and place and a map, if possible.

Company Name
Address
City, State Zip

Date

Name
Company Name
Address
City, State Zip

Dear

Please note that we have moved to a new location:

Company Name
Address
City, State Zip

Our new telephone number is: (212) 555-6789

Our previous address was:

Company Name
Address
City, State Zip

Please change your files to reflect this move.

Sincerely,

Name
Title

- Be sure to include your telephone number, even if it isn't new.

- Always include the previous address for reference.

Index by Title

Index by Subject

Job performance (*see also* Appraisals, job
    performance)
    memos regarding (7-12, 7-13), 226, 227
    written evaluation of (7-24, 7-25), 238,
        239, 240-241
Job skills
    outlined in job description (7-22, 7-23),
        236, 237
Jury duty
    requesting employee be excused from
        (8-10), 256

Landlord
    dealing with (8-09), 255
Lateness (*see also* Delays)
    explaining (9-07, 9-09), 272, 274
Leads
    letters generating (1-12, 1-13, 1-24), 14,
        15, 26
Lead time
    for submission of ads (2-06), 78
Leasing agreements (8-08, 8-09), 254, 255
Legal action
    notifying customer of, for nonpayment
        (5-16), 182
    responding to customer's threat of (4-19),
        163
Legal implications
    in personnel matters, **214**
Letters (*see also* Business form; Memos)
    full block (10-11, 10-12), 300, 301
    modified block (10-13, 10-14), 302, 303
Limited time offers
    use of, in store opening announcement
        (1-19), 21

Magazine advertising
    requesting rates for (2-06), 78
Managing your business, **245-246** (*see*
        Inquiries; Requests)
Maps
    use of, in trade show announcement (1-18),
        20
Marketing, **1-2** (*see also* Advertising, goals of;
        Advertising campaign)
    role of sales letter in, **1**
    use of questionnaires in (1-33), 35
Media (*see also* Broadcast advertising)
    procedures for dealing with (9-12, 9-19),
        278, 285
Meetings, **101** (*see also* Appointments)
    confirming (3-17), 119
    to discuss employee problem (7-13), 227

to discuss program development and cost
    (3-16), 118
to discuss services and fees (2-02, 2-17),
    74, 89
follow-up to (3-21), 123
notifying of (9-01), 265
recap of (9-04), 268-269
requesting associate attend (3-18), 120
rescheduling (3-23), 125
to review sales performance (1-31), 33
to submit quote (1-47), 52
Memos, **214, 263** (*see also* Reports)
    announcing assignments (9-03), 267
    announcing job opening (7-01), 215
    bad news (9-17), 283
    policy (9-13), 279
    procedure (9-12, 9-14), 278, 280
    recommendation (9-10, 9-11), 275, 276-277
    regarding benefits (7-21), 235
    regarding job performance (7-12, 7-13),
        226, 227
    requesting employee participation in charity
        drive (9-06), 271
    resignation (9-16), 282
    spacing in (10-01), 288
    thanking employee for suggestion (9-05),
        270
Merchandise
    being shipped (1-42), 47
    ready for pick-up (1-44), 49
    unavailable (1-40), 45
Messenger
    use of (1-54), 59
Motivation letter (7-28), 244 (*see also*
        Personnel relations)

Newspaper advertising
    requesting rates for (2-05), 77

Opening sentence
    and ''grabber,'' 1
Orders, **2**
    acknowledging (1-37, 1-38, 1-39, 1-40,
        1-41), 42, 43, 44, 45, 46
    canceling (6-13), 199
    received, unable to process (1-41), 46
    special, customer misunderstood terms of
        (4-14), 158
Ordering
    under consignment terms (1-61), 66
Outline
    format of (10-04), 291
Overnight service
    uses of (1-54), 59

Overpayment
   rectifying with refund check (3-35), 137

Payments
   cover letter for (6-19), 205
   crediting for (3-32), 134
   and customer dissatisfaction (4-13), 157
   debiting account, in lieu of (3-33), 135
   explaining delay in (6-21), 207
   inquiring about terms of (6-05), 191
   notifying of change in policy regarding
      (6-11), 197
   offering discounts for timely, **165**
   requesting additional, due to overlooked
      charges (3-34), 136
   withholding, until work or order is
      complete, (6-10, 6-11), 196, 197
Payment due, **102** (*see also* Collection letters)
   for goods received (1-46), 51
   on services rendered (1-45), 50
Performance (*see also* Warning memos to
      employees)
   appraising (10-05), 292–293
   complaining of unsatisfactory, to service
      company (6-14), 200
   regarding sales (1-31), 33
Personnel file (6-18), 204
Personnel relations, **213–214** (*see also*
      Benefits, employees; Employees; Job
      descriptions; Job offers; Job openings;
      Job performance)
   and business reverses (9-17, 9-18), 283,
      284
Policies
   announcing changes in (3-05, 6-11, 9-14),
      107, 197, 280
   recommending changes in (9-13), 279
Postscript
   use of, to generate response (1-32), 34
Premium
   use of, as incentive to new customer (1-17),
      19
Prepayments
   as discount option (1-16), 18
   requiring, after repeated delays in payment
      (3-31), 133
Press releases, **71–72**
   for anniversary celebration (2-26, 2-27),
      98, 99
   announcing employee achievement (2-23),
      95
   announcing merger (2-24), 96
   announcing new employee (2-22), 94
   announcing new partner (2-25), 97

announcing new product or product line
      (2-19, 2-20), 91, 92
   long version (2-27), 99
   short version (2-26), 98
Pricing
   explaining change in, to sales force (1-26),
      28
   notifying dealer of changes in (3-02, 3-03),
      104, 105
Probationary period, confirming, **214**
Procedures (*see also* Policies)
   announcement of new (9-14), 280
Products
   announcing new (1-25, 2-13, 2-19), 27, 85,
      91
   dealing with customer misunderstanding of
      (4-15), 159
   explaining, in sales letter (1-13, 1-25), 15,
      27
   inquiring about, to supplier (6-01), 187
   updating specifications of (1-27), 29
Profit and loss, statement of (*see* Income
      statements, format of)
Promotions, job
   announcing, **264,** (2-22, 9-15), 94, 281
   notifying of (7-26), 242
Promotions
   and relationships with ad agency (2-03),
      75
   of sales program (1-21, 1-22), 23, 24
   use of, in announcing opening of new
      branch or office (2-15), 87
   use of contest for (1-15), 17
   use of testimonials in (1-17), 19
Proposals, **2** (*see also* Quotations)
   enclosed in thank-you for opportunity to
      quote (1-48), 53
   follow-up to (1-51), 56
   sample of (1-50), 55
Public relations
   goals of, **71**
   hiring, firm (2-16), 88

Questionnaires
   consumer expo (1-36), 40–41
   cover letter for (1-32), 34
   to inactive client (1-35), 38–39
   about salespeople (1-34), 36–37
Quotations, **2** (*see also* Proposals)
   cover letter for (1-49), 54
   in flyer (1-14), 16
   rejecting (6-06), 192
   requesting (6-05), 191
   requesting opportunity to submit (1-47), 52

responding to request for, with questions (1-53), 58

Recommendations, **263**
  to adopt a course of action (9-11), 276–277
  to purchase equipment (9-10), 275
References, **214**
  checking, for credit approval (5-03, 5-04), 169, 170
  for employee who is leaving (7-15, 7-16), 229, 230
  for former employee (7-17), 231
  requesting (7-18), 232
  soliciting (1-10), 12
  thank-you for (1-11), 13
Refund
  for damaged goods (3-39), 141
Reports, **263–264**
  final (9-08), 273
  format of (10-02), 289
  progress (9-07), 272
Requests
  for list of attendees at meeting (3-22), 124
  for opportunity to quote (1-47), 52
  for payment covering returned check (3-25, 3-26, 3-27), 127, 128, 129
  to use name as reference (1-10), 12
Request to bid
  responses to (1-53), 58
Resignations
  announcing, **264,** (9-16), 282
Responses
  to request to bid (1-53), 58
  to request for information (1-09), 11
  to resume, with recommendation (7-04), 218
  to unsolicited resume (7-03), 217
Resumes
  response to, with referral (7-04), 218
  response to unsolicited (7-03), 217
Returned check
  requesting payment for (3-25, 3-26, 3-27), 127, 128, 129
Returns, **102**
  acknowledging, for credit (3-28), 140
  acknowledging, for exchange (3-37), 139
  when customer misunderstands product (4-15, 4-16, 4-17), 159, 160, 161
  of damaged goods (3-39), 141
  explaining changed policy regarding (3-05), 107
  of incorrect item (6-24), 210
  of item damaged in shipment (6-23), 209
  of non-returnable item (4-14), 158

tracing lost (3-40), 142
of unused merchandise, for credit (6-22), 208

Salary
  notification of increase (7-27), 243
Sales, **1–2** (*see also* Sales letters)
  use of contests in (1-15), 17
  use of flyers in (1-14), 16
  relationship of, to credit and collections, **165**
Sales calls
  arranging (1-12), 14
  follow-up to (1-05, 1-06), 7, 8
Sales campaign
  determining effectiveness of (1-19), 21
Sales force
  introducing addition to (1-28), 30
Sales letters, **1–2** (*see also* Sales)
  to follow up on sales call (1-05, 1-06), 7, 8
  to generate leads (1-12, 1-13), 14, 15
  to welcome new business (1-02), 4
  to welcome new client (1-03), 5
  to welcome new customer (1-04), 6
  to welcome new resident (1-01), 3
Salespeople
  communicating with, **2**
Sales territory
  explaining changed assignments in (1-29), 31
Samples
  use of, in letter to generate leads (1-13), 15
  use of, when requesting opportunity to quote (1-47), 52
Services
  explaining (1-12, 3-04), 14, 106
  requesting, under product warranty (6-08), 194
  role of questionnaire in improving (1-34, 1-35), 36–37, 38–39
Shipments, damaged
  apologizing for (4-06), 150
  returning item (6-23, 6-25), 209, 211
Shipment refused for quality reasons (6-09), 195
Shipping, **2**
  apologizing for delay in (4-04), 148
  errors in (1-06, 4-05), 8, 149
  explaining delay in (4-10), 154
  notifying of delay in (1-39), 44
Solicitations (*see also* Thank-you letter)
  to current customer, to increase business (1-07), 9
  to former customer (1-08), 10
  offering free estimates in (1-12), 14

NOTES

NOTES

NOTES

NOTES